ALLY McCOIST'S
QUESTION OF SOCCER

ALLY McCOIST'S
QUESTION OF SOCCER

ALLY McCOIST
with WILLIAM WALKER

CollinsWillow
An Imprint of HarperCollinsPublishers

First published in 1997
by CollinsWillow
an imprint of HarperCollins*Publishers*
London

1 3 5 7 9 8 6 4 2

A CIP catalogue record for this book is
available from the British Library

ISBN 0 00 218785 X

Front cover photograph supplied
courtesy of Rob Heath

Printed in Great Britain by
Caledonian International Book Manufacturing Ltd,
Glasgow

CONTENTS

CONTENTS

INTRODUCTION

As you may have noticed, I'm very fond of quizzes. I really enjoy pondering over questions like 'Name the Year', 'Who scored the goal?' and, one of my recent favourites, 'When is the manager going to put me on?'

Seriously though, while several players will say they're not concerned about history and statistics, I have to admit that setting records has always been a genuine source of satisfaction for me. I was especially delighted a couple of seasons back when I managed to beat Mr Bob McPhail's record of League goals for Rangers. That record had stood for 57 years and I'm as proud of beating it as I am of anything else I've achieved in the game.

Anyway, along with my research team-mate William Walker, I've been looking into some other footballing facts and feats and we've certainly unearthed plenty of interesting answers to questions on a vast range of topics.

So while I'm away having my anorak surgically removed, you can choose to either quiz your family and friends or perhaps just sit back and enjoy learning a few more stimulating facts about this great game.

All the best.

THE STORY OF FOOTBALL

In which country did football begin?
The ancestry of soccer can be traced all over the world. A
form of football, called *tsu chu* is mentioned in the writings
of the Chinese Han Dynasty while the ancient Romans and
Greeks also took part in ball sports. The Roman version
Harpastum was probably the forerunner of the early mob
football matches in medieval Britain.

What form did these matches take?
They appear to have begun as annual events in the days
leading up to Lent and basically consisted of two teams of
huge numbers attempting to propel a ball into the other
side's goal. The games were such unbelievably violent
affairs that householders had to barricade their lower
windows to protect themselves from the mobs. And I
thought Rangers-Celtic matches were tough!

What did they use for a ball?
A typical ball was made of leather stuffed with cork shavings
although the use of a pig's bladder is also recorded. In
Chester meanwhile, the locals were apparently content to
boot abcut the head of a defeated Viking invader!

What about the goals?
They varied from place to place. For the annual match at
Ashbourne in Derbyshire, the goals comprised two mill-
wheels, several MILES apart, while at Winchester School,
two boys stood at either end with their legs open! Gradually

however, custom-built goals in the form of two wooden posts came to be the norm.

So was a goal scored by forcing the ball between these posts?
Yes indeed and each goal was recorded by cutting a notch on one of the posts – that's where the term 'scoring a goal' comes from.

When did the game of football become more standardised?
The public schools and Cambridge University, in particular, take a lot of credit for installing some sort of order. The first serious attempt was the publishing of the Cambridge Rules in 1848.

When was the first football club established in Britain?
Some records state that the Sheffield Football Club was formed in 1855 while others give the date of foundation as 1857. Either way, it's claimed to be the oldest club in the world.

What about the Football Association – when did that come about?
The Football Association came into being in October 1863 following a meeting at the Freemasons Tavern in London. Its main purpose was to establish a code of rules for the game, but a serious split occurred over the acceptance of 'hacking'?

What was hacking exactly?
Hacking was the act of kicking an opponent on the leg. The hacking lobby, who also favoured handling, went on to develop their own game (which eventually evolved into

Rugby Union) while the dribbling code became known as
Association Football. The term 'soccer' is derived from the
word 'association'.

**And was the FA responsible for introducing regulated
competition?**
In 1866, the FA organised a match between the clubs of
Sheffield and London in Battersea Park. The game, won
comfortably by London, was the first representative match
in the history of football. Inter-county matches followed
and, in 1871, the FA Cup tournament began.

When did football develop into a spectator sport?
When the introduction of shorter working hours meant
more leisure time for Britain's factory workers, watching
football provided the ideal way to spend their newly freed
Saturday afternoons. Vast numbers clamoured to see their
local teams and bigger and bigger stadia were built to
accommodate them.

What about professionalism – when did that start?
The clubs were obviously making large sums of money from
admission charges and soccer was becoming a lucrative and
competitive business. Although the FA didn't formally
sanction professionalism until 1885, Glasgow man James
Lang is reputed to have become the first-ever professional
footballer when he was (allegedly!) paid to play for Sheffield
Wednesday in 1876.

So how did football spread to the rest of the world?
Britain was a major world power in the late 19th century
and, as communication and travel developed, its influence
spread to all corners of the globe. British sailors, soldiers,
businessmen and teachers took their sport with them and it

wasn't long before the locals were joining them in their kick-abouts. By the turn of the century, football clubs were flourishing all over Europe and South America.

DID YOU KNOW?

⚽ Dynamo Moscow were founded by English mill owners Clement and Harry Charnock.

⚽ The famous Brazilian club Corinthians are called after the celebrated English amateur team of the same name.

⚽ Juventus based their trademark black-and-white striped jersey on Notts County's strip.

⚽ Argentina's most successful club, River Plate, was founded in 1901 by British residents of Buenos Aires.

⚽ AC Milan actually started life as the Milan Cricket and Football Club in 1899. That's why the club still use the English city-name rather than the Italian Milano.

THE FA CUP

When was the FA Cup first contested?
The first tournament was held in 1871–72 and was won by a team called The Wanderers. They defeated Royal Engineers in the final.

Has the final always been staged at Wembley?
No. Wembley wasn't built until 1923. The early finals were held at Kennington Oval which is now better known as a cricket ground.

There was crowd trouble at the first Wembley final, wasn't there?
In a manner of speaking. There was the slight problem of 200,000 people cramming into a ground which, at that time, was supposed to hold 126,000. Amazingly, the pitch was cleared by a mounted policeman on a white horse and Bolton went on to defeat West Ham 2–0.

Which team has won the FA Cup most often?
Manchester United have lifted the trophy on nine occasions. The Reds first won the tournament in 1909 when they defeated Bristol City in the final.

Is it true that Everton have played in more semi-finals than any other club?
Yes. The Merseyside men have reached the last four on 23 separate occasions. On 12 of these, they went through to the final.

Has any player ever scored a hat-trick in the final?
There have been three: Billy Townley (Blackburn Rovers,
1890), Jimmy Logan (Notts County, 1894) and Stan
Mortensen (Blackpool, 1953). Of these only Mortensen's
was scored at Wembley.

Has a non-League side ever won the FA Cup?
Tottenham Hotspur were still a Southern League club when
they won the competition in 1901. However, they weren't
really a non-League club as we would understand it today,
just not yet part of the professional set-up which was based
in the North and Midlands.

**When was the Cup last won by a team from outside of the
top division?**
West Ham were in the old Second Division when they
defeated Arsenal 1–0 to take the trophy in 1980. Trevor
Brooking, now better known as a BBC pundit, headed the
game's only goal.

**Chesterfield did well with their FA Cup run of 1996–97.
Has a team from the lower divisions ever played in the
final?**
No, but six clubs from the old Third Division have appeared
in the semi-final. They were Millwall (1937), Port Vale (1954),
York (1955), Norwich (1959), Crystal Palace (1976) and
Plymouth (1984).

**What has been the highest number of matches needed to
decide an FA Cup tie?**
The 1971–72 Alvechurch v Oxford City fourth qualifying
round tie required SIX games before Alvechurch eventually
triumphed 1–0.

**Who was the player who scored six goals in an FA Cup tie
but still finished on the losing side?**
That was Denis Law who bagged all six for Manchester City
in a 6–2 win at Luton in 1961. Unfortunately for Denis, the
match was abandoned and Luton won the replay!

**Apart from abandoned matches etc., has a team ever lost a
game but still won the competition?**
No. However in 1945–46, the tournament was played on a
two-leg, home-and-away basis and Charlton Athletic
reached the final having gone down 2–1 to Fulham in a
second leg tie.

What's the biggest upset in FA Cup history?
The tournament has produced countless shock results over
the years. Two of the biggest include Newcastle's 1972
defeat at Hereford and Sutton's win over Coventry in 1989. I
doubt also if my old club Sunderland were too chuffed about
their 2–1 loss at Yeovil in 1949!

**Has a team ever won the tournament after being drawn
AWAY in every round?**
Arsenal (in 1971) and Manchester United (in 1990) have
both achieved this impressive feat.

Is Ian Rush the leading FA scorer of all time?
No. Rushie's goal for Liverpool against Rochdale in January
1996 was his 42nd in the competition and enough to
overtake Denis Law as the leading scorer THIS CENTURY.
Notts County's Henry Cursham still holds the overall record
with 48 between 1880 and 1887.

I've heard something to the effect that Sunderland and Arsenal BOTH won the FA Cup in the SAME year. Surely that can't be right?
Well, it's sort of right. In 1979, striker *Alan* Sunderland scored the goal which won the Cup for Arsenal.

I've also heard a question about items which are taken to the FA Cup Final every year but never used. What's the answer to that one?
This is a sneaky one. It's the ribbons in the colours of the losing team!

ALLY'S TOP TEN

Ten Scots who have captained FA Cup winning sides …

Alex James (Arsenal, 1936)
Tom Smith (Preston, 1938)
Jimmy Scoular (Newcastle, 1955)
Ron Yeats (Liverpool, 1965)
Dave Mackay (Tottenham, 1967)
Frank McLintock (Arsenal, 1971)
Billy Bremner (Leeds, 1972)
Bobby Kerr (Sunderland, 1973)
Martin Buchan (Manchester United, 1977)
Alan Hansen (Liverpool, 1986)

THE PREMIERSHIP

When did the FA Premiership begin?
The FA Premiership, originally called the FA Premier League, began in 1992 when the Football Association took over the running of what had been the old Football League First Division. The competition became known as the FA Carling Premiership in 1993.

Why was it set up?
Basically, because the leading clubs were keen to acquire a bigger share of TV revenue. The £304 million, five-year deal struck between the Premier League and BSkyB in 1992 was the most lucrative in British sporting history.

What other changes came about?
The FA administrators claimed they would make the England team a priority and ensure more free weekends to allow the international players to prepare.

Who scored the first-ever Premiership goal?
Brian Deane for Sheffield United against Manchester United at Bramall Lane on 15 August 1992.

What's the highest victory ever recorded in the Premiership?
That was Manchester United's 9–0 win over Ipswich in March 1995. Andy Cole banged in five goals in that game – a record haul by one player. The biggest away victory is Nottingham Forest's 7–1 triumph at Sheffield Wednesday in April 1995.

Who was the first player to score 100 Premiership goals?
Alan Shearer (surprise, surprise!) who reached the ton
when he hit Blackburn's winning goal against Tottenham at
Ewood Park in December 1995.

**In how many seasons has Alan Shearer finished as the top
scorer in the Premiership?**
Alan was the leading marksman in three consecutive
seasons: 1994–95, 1995–96 and 1996–97. The 34 goals he
scored in 1994–95 equalled the record set by Andy Cole
during 1993–94 for most goals in a single Premiership
season.

**What is the record points total achieved by a Premiership
team?**
Manchester United notched 92 points in their first 'Double'
season of 1993–94. That total was accumulated from 42
games rather than the current standard 38.

**Manchester United won four of the first five Premier
League titles. How many players appeared in all four
winning teams?**
Peter Schmeichel, Denis Irwin, Gary Pallister, Brian McClair,
Ryan Giggs, Nicky Butt and Eric Cantona all turned out in
each of the victorious Premiership seasons.

**United clinched the 1997 championship without kicking a
ball. Is that the first time that's happened?**
No. In 1993, Aston Villa's 1–0 home defeat by Oldham
guaranteed that United were champions while, the following
season, Blackburn conceded the title to The Reds after
going down 2–1 at Coventry.

Has the Premier League always contained 20 clubs?
There were 22 teams in the original line-up in 1992. In 1995, the number was reduced to 20 when four clubs were relegated and only two promoted.

What's the most dramatic finish to a Premiership relegation battle?
In 1993–94, Everton produced a real Houdini-act to survive, coming back from 2–0 down to win 3–2 in their final match at home to Wimbledon. Sheffield United, meanwhile, took the drop after losing a late goal at Chelsea.

How many teams have been Premiership ever-presents since 1992?
I make it 13 – Arsenal, Aston Villa, Blackburn, Chelsea, Coventry, Everton, Leeds, Liverpool, Manchester United, Tottenham, Sheffield Wednesday, Southampton and Wimbledon.

THE FOOTBALL LEAGUE

How did the Football League come about?
By the late 1880s, professional football was commonplace
and clubs needed gate revenue to meet their hefty wage
bills. Although the FA Cup had been running since 1871,
friendly matches were unable to provide a sufficient amount
of regular income.

So what did the clubs do about it?
Would you believe a Scotsman, a Perthshire man called
William McGregor, was the man behind the idea of a set
programme of fixtures. McGregor was a member of Aston
Villa and he wrote to several other clubs with his plan.

When did the League start?
In March 1888, a meeting took place at London's Anderton's
Hotel (maybe the owner was a relation of Darren!) and
matches began in September that year.

How many clubs were originally members?
Twelve – Accrington, Blackburn Rovers, Bolton, Burnley,
Everton and Preston North End (all from Lancashire) plus
six from the Midlands – Aston Villa, Derby, Notts County,
Stoke, West Bromwich Albion and Wolves. No southern
clubs were involved since there was no professional football
south of Birmingham.

So which team scored the first-ever Football League goal?
That's credited to Preston when Jack Gordon netted against
Burnley. The team went from strength to strength and took
the 22-game championship without losing a single match.

Nicknamed 'The Invincibles', Preston also lifted the 1889 FA Cup, becoming the first side to win the coveted 'Double'.

When did a Second Division come into being?

In 1892, a grouping of clubs called the Football Alliance was absorbed by the League to become the Second Division. By the turn of the century, the League had expanded to include 18 clubs in each of its two divisions.

Who were the first teams to be promoted and relegated?

Lancashire-based Darwen were relegated into the new Second Division in 1892. However, the following season they became one of the first clubs to be promoted when they defeated Notts County in a play-off (or Test-match as it was then known). Sheffield United also moved up after beating Accrington. Ironically, Small Heath (later to be Birmingham City) finished top of the inaugural Second Division championship but missed out on promotion after losing their test match against Newton Heath.

When were Divisions Three and Four formed?

The Third Division was created at the start of 1920–21 when practically the entire Southern League joined the League as 'Associate' members. Crystal Palace won the first championship and, the following season, the Third Division split into regionalized North and South sections. In 1958, the two sections merged to become Football League Divisions Three and Four.

Which team has won the English League Championship most often?

Liverpool still lead the way with 18 titles between 1901 and 1990. Manchester United come next with 11 (that's including their four FA Premiership victories since 1993).

What's the record number of consecutive championship wins by one club?
No club has beaten the three-in-a-row recorded by Huddersfield Town (1924–26), Arsenal (1933–35) and Liverpool (1982–84).

Were Arsenal the first London club to win the championship?
Yes, but surprisingly that was not until 1931. The Gunners have proved the capital's most successful club overall with 10 victories, the last being in 1991. Tottenham have managed two championships while Chelsea, in 1955, are the only other London side to have won it.

Which player has the most championship medals?
Both Phil Neal and Alan Hansen won eight titles with Liverpool. Kenny Dalglish has been involved with nine championship winning sides – eight at Liverpool and one as manager of Blackburn.

Which clubs have won the League and FA Cup 'Double'?
Preston (1889), Aston Villa (1897), Tottenham (1961), Arsenal (1971) and Manchester United, twice (1994 and 1996).

Has any team played in all of England's variously-named divisions?
Yes. Coventry City appeared in all six divisions of the old-style Football League and have been FA Premier League ever-presents since 1992.

Has any club ever won the League Championship and then been relegated the following season?
Amazingly, in 1937–38, Manchester City took the drop just twelve months after securing their first title. Oh dear!

Which was the first club to automatically lose its League status as a result of finishing last in the bottom division?
Lincoln City in 1986–87. They bounced back the following year however by winning the Vauxhall Conference.

Are the play-offs a relatively modern thing?
Yes, the previously-mentioned 'Test matches' were abolished in 1897 and automatic promotion and relegation was the norm until the play-offs were re-introduced in 1987. From 1987 to 1988, the team just above the drop zone in the higher division competed with the three sides immediately below the automatic promotion places in the lower league.

THE LEAGUE CUP

When did the competition become known as the Coca-Cola Cup?
Coca-Cola took over the sponsorship of the tournament in 1992. Prior to that it had been variously the Rumbelows Cup, the Littlewoods Cup and the Milk Cup.

Has it always been a sponsored tournament?
No, the first sponsors were the Milk Marketing Board in 1981. The tournament itself actually goes back to the 1960–61 season.

Whose idea was it?
The League Cup was the brainchild of Alan Hardaker, the long-serving and influential secretary of the Football League. Just like today, many of the big clubs condemned the tournament as ill-conceived and a burden on an already over-loaded season.

Who were the first winners?
Aston Villa overcame Rotherham in the first final which was played over two legs.

So the final wasn't always held at Wembley?
No, Wembley staged its first League Cup final in 1967 when Queens Park Rangers, then in Division Three, defeated First Division West Bromwich Albion 3–2 in a pulsating match.

Did the Wembley final change the attitude of the big clubs to the tournament?
Apparently, and what was also very important to its success

was the decision made by the League in 1966 to award a European Fairs Cup place to any First Division team which won the trophy. With the exception of Liverpool and Everton, all the top clubs entered the 1966–67 tournament.

Which team has won the League Cup most often?
Aston Villa and Liverpool have each won it on five occasions between 1961 and 1997.

Which player holds the record for the most winner's medals?
Ian Rush has five League Cup badges from his Liverpool days. Both Rushie and Kenny Dalglish appeared in six finals with the Anfield side.

Leicester and Middlesbrough had to replay the 1997 Coca-Cola Cup final. Was that the first occasion that an additional match was required?
No, there had been several replays before that. In 1984, Liverpool defeated Everton in a replay at Maine Road and, in 1981, they beat West Ham 2–1 at Villa Park. In 1978, the Reds lost a return match with Nottingham Forest while, in the previous year, Aston Villa eventually overcame Everton 3–2 in a second replay.

What's the biggest victory ever recorded in a League Cup final?
Norwich defeated Fourth Division Rochdale 4–0 on aggregate in the 1962 final but the largest single-match wins are the 3–0 victories of Oxford (v QPR) in 1986 and Aston Villa (v Leeds) in 1996.

Has the tournament ever witnessed any crazy results?
West Ham trounced Bury 10–0 in a second leg tie during

1983 while Fulham crashed 10–0 in a 1986 first leg match at
Liverpool. Interestingly, the Fulham programme for the
second leg is reputed to have printed details of the extra-
time arrangements. Now, that's what I call optimism!

What about individual performances?
Oldham's Frankie Bunn slammed in six goals against
Scarborough in a 1989 tie while the best seasonal League
Cup haul was Clive Allen's 12 strikes in nine appearances for
Tottenham during 1986–87.

**What about the 'Double' of League and League Cup. Has
that ever been achieved?**
Nottingham Forest were the first club to do it in 1978.
Liverpool managed to lift the League Cup during every
season of their three consecutive championship victories
between 1982 and 1984. In 1993, Arsenal became the first
team to win the League and FA Cups in the same season.

ALLY'S TOP TEN

Ten Scots who have scored in English League Cup finals…

Eddie McCreadie (Chelsea v Leicester City, 1965)
John Robertson (Nottingham Forest v Liverpool, 1978 replay)
Andy Gray (Wolves v Nottingham Forest, 1980)
Ray Stewart (West Ham v Liverpool, 1981)
Kenny Dalglish (Liverpool v West Ham, 1981 replay)
Steve Archibald (Tottenham v Liverpool, 1982)
Graeme Souness (Liverpool v Everton, 1984 replay)
Gordon Chisholm (own goal for Norwich v Sunderland, 1985)
Charlie Nicholas (Arsenal v Liverpool, 1987)
Brian McClair (Manchester United v Nottingham Forest, 1992)

GOING CLUBBING

Which is the oldest club on Merseyside?
Everton who were founded in 1878. They actually played at
Anfield between 1884 and 1892 when they left after a
disagreement with their landlord. The landlord decided to
form his own club which eventually became Liverpool FC.
Tranmere Rovers, who play across the river in Birkenhead,
were founded in 1884.

**Manchester United have been the front-runners in English
football in recent seasons but have Manchester City ever
been the dominant force in the area?**
United have really been Manchester's senior side since the
1900s but there have been a few spells in which City
outshone their more illustrious rivals. The most notable
period was in the late 1960s and early '70s when, under the
management of Joe Mercer, the Sky Blues lifted the
Championship, FA Cup, League Cup and European Cup-
Winners' Cup within the space of three seasons.

**What is the highest number of London clubs in England's
top division in a single season?**
All of the capital's 12 clubs (that's not including Watford and
Barnet) played in the old-style First Division at some stage.
The highest London representation in a single top flight
season was eight teams during 1989–90.

**Which has been the more successful of the Sheffield
clubs?**
That would appear to be Wednesday who have won four
championships, three FA Cups and one League Cup. Rivals

27

United can only claim one League title (1897–98) although they have won four FA Cups. Wednesday have also been Premier League ever-presents since 1992.

What is the most remotely situated League club in England?
I think that must be Carlisle United who are 58 miles from their nearest rivals, Newcastle United. It's been calculated however that Plymouth Argyle have the longest average journey time when travelling to away matches.

Several clubs have launched share issues in recent seasons. Which was the first British club to 'go public' on the stock exchange?
Tottenham Hotspur in 1983. Later in the decade, Hibernian became the first Scottish club to 'float'.

Which of the Welsh clubs have played in England's top division?
Cardiff City have had three spells in the old First Division while Swansea, between 1981 and 1983, were the most recent Welsh representatives in the top flight.

Have any Scottish clubs ever played in the English League?
No, although several have competed in the FA Cup tournament, including Rangers (in 1886–87) and, much more recently, Gretna. On the other hand, Scottish League side Berwick Rangers are actually based in England.

Which is Scotland's oldest football club?
Queen's Park who were founded in 1867 and still play their home matches at Hampden Park.

Livingston appeared on the Scottish scene during the past couple of seasons. Are they a brand new club?
No, they are the club formerly known as Meadowbank Thistle and simply re-named themselves when they moved from Edinburgh to their new home town in 1995. Meadowbank joined the Scottish League in 1974, having been previously called Ferranti Thistle.

So where do St Johnstone and St Mirren come from?
St Johnstone, my first senior club, are based in Perth (once known as St John's Toun) while St Mirren hail from Paisley and are named after the town's patron saint .

Which was the last club to quit the Football League?
That was Maidstone United in August 1992. Known as 'The Stones' they had only won promotion from the Vauxhall Conference as recently as 1989 and it was sad that a financial crisis (plus the absence of their own home ground) forced them into extinction.

THE SCOTTISH LEAGUE

How many times have Rangers now won the Scottish League championship?
Our ninth consecutive title in 1996–97 was the club's 47th overall – a clear world record apparently.

How many championships have Celtic won?
Celtic have been champions on 35 occasions and I'll sportingly mention that they also won nine-in-a-row between 1966 and 1974!

So who's the best of the rest?
Aberdeen, Hearts and Hibs all have four title wins to their credit. However, the League flag has not flown in the capital since Hearts won it in 1960.

Did Rangers win the first-ever Scottish championship?
They actually shared it with Dumbarton. The teams finished level on points and a play-off to decide the title ended in a 2–2 draw.

When did the Premier League begin?
The new ten-team Premier League started in season 1975–76. Rangers defeated Celtic 2–1 in their first match and went on to win the inaugural championship.

Has the Premier League always featured ten clubs?
No, from 1986 to 1988 and from 1991 to 1994, it was a twelve-club league. That meant that each team played a very tiring 44 match programme.

How many teams have won the Premier division since 1976?

Only four – Rangers, Celtic, Aberdeen and Dundee United. United's victory in 1982–83 was a tremendous achievement for manager Jim McLean and his assistant at that time, Walter Smith.

What's the tightest finish to a Scottish League championship race?

There have been several nail-biters but arguably the most dramatic finales came in 1991 and 1965. In 1991, Rangers defeated Aberdeen 2–0 in a last day do-or-die battle while, in 1965, Kilmarnock travelled to Edinburgh to defeat Hearts 2–0 and pip the Tynecastle side on goal average.

Did Hearts not lose the title on goal DIFFERENCE during the 1980s?

Yes they did. On the final day of 1985–86, long-term leaders Hearts crashed 2–0 at Dundee while Celtic were trouncing St Mirren 5–0 at Paisley to take the championship. Ironically, the Jam Tarts would have won in 1986 if goal average had still been in use while goal difference (not introduced until 1970) would have given them the 1965 championship.

Apart from the Old Firm, which teams have been Premier League ever-presents since 1975?

Aberdeen are the only other perpetual members of the top flight but they came perilously close to going down in 1995. The Dons needed a play-off victory over Dunfermline to retain their status.

Are the play-offs a relatively new thing in Scottish football?

Yes, they were introduced in 1994–95 and only involve the

second bottom team in the Premier and the First Division runners-up. All the other Scottish divisions are two-up/two-down.

Has the Scottish League, like its English counterpart, lost many clubs over the years?
Quite a few. Some famous names from the early days are either no longer with us or operating as minor league teams. They include Clydesdale, Cowlairs, Leith Athletic, St Bernards and Vale of Leven. The biggest loss was probably Third Lanark, a famous Glasgow club which folded in 1967. Andy Goram's dad, Lewis, once played for them as did former Scotland boss Ally MacLeod.

How many Scottish League clubs are there now?
There were 40 at the end of 1996–97. Former Highland League sides Ross County and Inverness Caledonian Thistle were invited to join in 1994–95 enabling the league to be restructured into four divisions of ten.

Has any club played in all four divisions?
One-time Premier League outfit Dumbarton became the first to do this when they dropped into Division Three in 1997.

DID YOU KNOW?

⚽ The *Scottish Sport* newspaper didn't exactly welcome the formation of the Scottish League in 1890. 'It stinks of finance, money-making and money-grabbing,' protested the *Sport*.

⚽ Only 80 people turned up for the Second Division match between Meadowbank Thistle and Stenhousemuir in

December 1979. The stay-aways didn't miss much as the game ended 0–0.

⚽ Celtic defeated Raith Rovers 6–0 and Motherwell 3–1 on the SAME DAY in April 1916.

⚽ On 9 February 1963, the ENTIRE Scottish League programme was wiped out by snow and ice.

THE SCOTTISH CUP

Who won the first Scottish Cup?
Queen's Park who defeated Clydesdale FC 2–0 in the final at
the original Hampden Park. The famous Glasgow amateur
club won six of the first nine tournaments.

Which team has won the cup most often?
Celtic lead the way with 30 victories to Rangers' 27.
Cup wins have been shared around a lot more than
championship successes and 23 different clubs have had
their name on the trophy.

Has any side ever managed three consecutive triumphs?
Yes, Queen's Park, Vale of Leven, Rangers and Aberdeen
have all accomplished this. The Dons were the most recent
team to do it, from 1982 to 1984.

**What's the record for consecutive appearances in the
final?**
Rangers' eight successive final appearances between 1976
and 1983 is the all-time record for the tournament.

What was the biggest Scottish Cup upset of all time?
Although Falkirk's 1997 semi-final win over Celtic was
certainly a surprise, it can't compare with Rangers'
humbling defeat at the hands of Second Division Berwick in
1967. Interestingly enough, my old Ibrox gaffer Jock Wallace
was player-manager for the Borderers that day.

Rangers demolished Hearts 5–1 in the 1996 final. Is that the biggest score in the final?

No, Renton defeated Cambuslang 6–1 in 1888 and Celtic beat Hibs by the same score in 1972. In 1934 meanwhile, Rangers won 5–0 against St Mirren.

What about the highest score recorded in early round games?

Only one winner there – Arbroath's 36–0 victory over the Aberdeen-based team Bon Accord in 1885 is in fact a WORLD RECORD score for ANY football match. More recently, Stirling Albion managed to ease past Selkirk by 20–0 in 1984!

How many times have Glasgow's Old Firm met in the final?

The Big Two have faced each other on 13 occasions between 1894 and 1989. Rangers triumphed in the first meeting but Celtic lead this particular contest with seven wins to five. The cup was withheld after the 1909 Old Firm final.

Why was that?

After the final replay had finished 1–1, the fans were incensed that extra-time was not to played. A four-hour riot ensued in which the supporters tore down barricades, lit bonfires and fought with police. Things are a bit quieter nowadays – believe me!

Has any player ever won Scottish Cup medals with BOTH Old Firm clubs?

The last player to achieve this rare distinction was Alfie Conn who, coincidentally, won both his medals in Old Firm finals. Alfie scored for Rangers in their 3–2 victory over Celtic in 1973 and, four years later, was in the Hoops side which defeated the Gers 1–0.

Kilmarnock and Falkirk contested the 1997 final. How many years was it since neither Rangers nor Celtic were represented?

The last Old Firm-free final was the Motherwell-Dundee United match of 1991. The game turned out to be an absolute cracker with 'Well, managed at the time by Tommy McLean, defeating his brother Jim's United side 4–3 after extra-time.

Dundee United lost in several finals before they eventually won the trophy. How many was it?

Jim McLean led the Tangerines to SIX losing finals before he was succeeded as manager by the Serbian, Ivan Golac, in 1993. Then, amazingly, the former Southampton star lifted the cup in his first season as boss!

I've heard something about a team scoring a Scottish Cup final goal BEFORE three o'clock. That can't be right surely?

It's absolutely true! In 1976, the Rangers-Hearts match kicked off a minute early and my good pal, Derek Johnstone, headed the Gers into the lead after just 45 seconds of play.

Is it true that Rangers once failed to turn up for a Scottish Cup final?

Yes, in 1879 the club decided not to contest the final replay with Vale of Leven since they felt aggrieved that a poor refereeing decision had robbed them of victory in the first match. The players went on a trip to Ayr Races instead!

THE SCOTTISH
LEAGUE CUP

**Did the Scottish League Cup begin at the same time as the
League Cup in England?**
No. The Scottish League Cup was first contested in season
1946–47. Rangers won the inaugural tournament by
defeating Aberdeen 4–0 in the final.

Was it always a straight knock-out format?
No. Until 1977–78, the early rounds consisted of league-style
sections with four or five teams playing each other twice.

Have Rangers won the tournament most often?
Yes. Our 4–3 victory over Hearts in November 1996 was the
club's 20th success in the competition. I've been fortunate
enough to have gained nine winners' medals myself which is
a record by one player.

**Celtic had a great side in the 1960s and early '70s. How did
they fare in the League Cup?**
Under their legendary manager Jock Stein, the Celts
reached an amazing 14 consecutive finals between 1964 and
1978. They only won six of them however.

**Derek Johnstone was just a youngster when he scored
Rangers' winning goal in the 1970 final. What age was he?**
Derek was still only 16 when he rose above veteran Celtic
skipper Billy McNeill to head a fabulous goal. That victory
ended Rangers' longest trophy-less spell since the war.

Is it right that a player once scored a hat-trick in the final yet still finished on the losing side?

That's exactly what happened to Joe Harper in 1974. He bagged all three goals for Hibs who lost 6–3 to Celtic.

Why were Dundee allowed to play the 1980 final on their own ground?

Since both Dundee clubs had reached the final, the League decided that the match should be contested in the city itself. A coin-toss determined that the game was staged at Dundee's Dens Park, although in the end home advantage proved insignificant as Dundee United cruised to a 3–0 victory.

Who was the player who appeared in the Scottish League Cup Final and the English FA Cup Final in the same season?

That was Gordon Smith in 1982–83. Gordon played on loan for Rangers in the Scottish League Cup final in December and later appeared for Brighton against Manchester United at Wembley in May. Unfortunately, he was a loser in both finals.

How did Rangers manage to win two League Cup Finals during 1984?

This was because the 1983–84 final was held in March and the 1984–85 final took place in October. Our 1983–84 match against Celtic was the first major Scottish final to be staged on a Sunday.

Apart from the Old Firm, which club has won the tournament most often?

Aberdeen have enjoyed five triumphs while Hearts have won it on four occasions. Interestingly, lowly East Fife were the first team to lift the trophy three times. The Fifers had a useful side in the late 1940s and early '50s.

What's the biggest score ever chalked up in the competition?

Ayr United defeated Dumbarton 11–1 in August 1952 while Partick Thistle also won 11–1 in their away tie against Albion Rovers in August 1993. SEVEN different Thistle players were on the scoresheet that night.

What's the tournament's biggest shock result?

Many people would say First Division Raith Rovers' victory over Celtic in the 1994 final although Partick Thistle's 4–1 win against the Celts in 1971 was also a huge surprise at the time.

Celtic once beat Rangers 7–1 in a League Cup final. When was that?

Next question please! I believe it was in 1957 although fortunately we don't see it very often. The BBC missed five of the goals after a technician left a dust cover on the camera lens!

ALLY'S TOP TEN

Ten Old Firm Scottish League Cup finals since 1957…

Rangers 2 Celtic 1 (1964–65)
Celtic 2 Rangers 1 (1965–66)
Celtic 1 Rangers 0 (1966–67)
Rangers 1 Celtic 0 (1970–71)
Rangers 1 Celtic 0 (1975–76)
Rangers 2 Celtic 1 (1977–78)
Celtic 2 Rangers 1 (1982–83)
Rangers 3 Celtic 2 (1983–84)
Rangers 2 Celtic 1 (1986–87)
Rangers 2 Celtic 1 (1990–91)

RANGERS: MY TEAM

How did the club begin?
Rangers were founded around 1873 by a group of lads from
Argyllshire who were working in Glasgow. They were
originally keen rowers but the new sport of football soon
captured their imagination.

Why the name 'Rangers'?
The club are actually called after an English RUGBY side.
Founder Moses McNeil came across the name while reading
C.W. Alcock's *English Football Annual* and his suggestion was
unanimously accepted by the other club members.

Have they always played in blue?
Moses and his mates chose blue and white as the team
colours and, after a brief spell during 1882–83 when they
wore blue and white hooped jerseys, the Gers eventually
settled into their established kit of blue shirts, white shorts
and the famous black socks with red tops.

And has Ibrox always been the club's home?
The first Rangers matches were played on Glasgow Green
which is in the east central part of the city. They then moved
west to Burnbank (off Great Western Road) and south to
Kinning Park before settling in the Ibrox area in 1887.

When was the first Rangers v Celtic match?
That came in May 1888 and it was also Celtic's first-ever
game. A crowd of 2,000 watched them defeat the Gers 5–2.

What is Rangers' best result against their old rivals?
Our 5–1 win at Ibrox in August 1988 was the club's biggest

victory in the Old Firm fixture since a previous 5–1 triumph at Parkhead in September 1960. Rangers' biggest-ever victory was 8–1 on 1 January 1943 but, being a wartime match, is sadly considered unofficial!

The Gers defeated Celtic in all four league meetings during 1996–97. Is that the first time that's happened?
Yes, neither team had previously whitewashed the other in league matches since the Premier Division began in 1975. In 1963–64, the Old Firm met five times (three in cup ties) with the boys in blue winning all five games.

What is Rangers' best performance in European competition?
Led by inspirational captain John Greig, the Gers lifted the 1972 European Cup-Winners' Cup by defeating Moscow Dynamo in Barcelona. That was the club's third appearance in the final of that tournament – they had lost to Fiorentina of Italy in 1961 and Bayern Munich in 1967.

What about the Champions' Cup?
Rangers reached the semi-final in 1960, losing 12–4 on aggregate to Eintracht Frankfurt. Our 1993 Champions League return match in Marseille was also a virtual semi-final since, had we won, we would have gone through to the final against Milan.

What is the greatest Rangers team of all time?
That's obviously a matter of opinion but certainly the record of the championship team of 1898–99 is hard to top. They won ALL 18 of their Scottish League matches, scoring 79 goals and conceding 18.

Have the Gers ever been relegated?
Never. The club's lowest-ever finishing position in the Scottish League is sixth, in 1925–26.

The arrival of Graeme Souness had a big influence on Rangers fortunes during the 1980s. How much of a difference did he make?

A massive difference. His reputation immediately raised the profile of the club and he was able to attract top quality players like Terry Butcher and Chris Woods. In Graeme Souness's first season in charge, the team won more Premier League matches than in the previous two seasons TOGETHER.

He signed a lot of players from England. How many altogether?

Graeme brought 18 English players to Ibrox during his five years as Rangers boss. He actually signed more Englishmen than Scots and the side which defeated Hearts to clinch the 1989 Premier League championship contained no less than SEVEN English players.

Walter Smith has been involved in nine championship successes. Is he the most successful Rangers manager of all time?

It's difficult to compare different eras but I would have though that Walter will be able to stake a good claim. However, an unbelievable total of 18 championships were won under the management of Bill Struth.

Who's Rangers most famous fan?

The club can count several big names amongst its supporters. They include pop stars Lulu and Wet Wet Wet, golfers Sam Torrance and Colin Montgomerie, rugby heroes Gavin Hastings and Craig Chalmers and even newsreaders Alistair Burnet and Kirsty Young. Scots movie legend Sean Connery, a close friend of Ibrox chairman David Murray, has also been to watch the team on several occasions.

THE WORLD CUP

The World Cup trophy that England won in 1966 was called the 'Jules Rimet Trophy'. Who was Jules Rimet?
Rimet was a French lawyer and President of FIFA from 1920 to 1954. It was he, along with fellow countryman Henri Delaunay, who came up with the idea of a world football championship.

When was the World Cup first contested?
The first tournament took place in 1930 in Uruguay. Since a lengthy boat journey was involved, only four European countries entered – France, Belgium, Romania and Yugoslavia. The Romanian team was actually picked by their monarch, King Carol, who also arranged that the players received time off work.

Who were the first winners?
Uruguay defeated their old rivals Argentina 4–2 in an exciting final in Montevideo. The Argentinians brought thousands of fans with them on specially-chartered boats.

Which was the first European country to win the World Cup?
The 1934 tournament was staged in Italy and the hosts lifted the cup by defeating Czechoslovakia in the final, 2–1 after extra-time. The victory was seen as a propaganda boost for the government of the country's Fascist dictator, Mussolini. Italy retained the trophy in France four years later.

When did the home nations first enter the tournament?
The British Home International Championship was used as

qualifying competition for the 1950 World Cup and England topped the section to reach the finals in Brazil. FIFA also invited runners-up Scotland but they declined because they had not won the group!

How did England fare?
Eh, not too well. Although they beat Chile, they lost to Spain and, almost incredibly, went down 1–0 to the part-timers of the USA!

Did Brazil win that tournament?
No, surprisingly they didn't. In front of a huge crowd in the newly-built Maracana Stadium, Uruguay sensationally beat them 2–1 in the deciding match. There were a few tears shed that night!

So when did Brazil first win the World Cup?
Brazil had to wait until 1958 in Sweden to get their hands on the trophy. A 17-year-old called Pelé was the main man as the Samba Stars defeated the hosts 5–2 in an absorbing final. They followed that with another triumph in Chile in 1962.

Bobby and Jack Charlton both played in England's victorious side of 1966. Are they the only brothers to have appeared in the World Cup final?
No, the first brothers to win a World Cup medal were West Germany's Fritz and Ottmar Walter in 1954 but, 24 years earlier, Argentina's losing side included the Evaristo brothers, Juan and Mario. Two other pairs of brothers have played in the final – Willy and Rene Van de Kerkhof (Holland, 1978) and Bernd and Karlheinz Forster (West Germany, 1982).

Have there ever been any 'repeat' finals?
West Germany v Argentina in 1990 was a re-match of the
1986 final. The 1994 finalists Brazil and Italy had met in the
deciding game of the 1970 tournament.

**Why was Diego Maradona's quarter-final goal against
England in 1986 known as the 'Hand of God' goal?**
After the match, the Argentinian star claimed that the goal
had been scored by 'a little bit the head of Maradona and a
little bit the Hand of God'. It was his way of saying that he
punched the ball into the net.

**Has a country ever won the World Cup after losing a
match?**
Yes, West Germany were the first to do this in 1954. They
were actually trounced 8–3 by favourites Hungary in a pool
match before they went on to defeat Puskas and Co. 3–2 in
the final. In 1974, West Germany lost a group match to East
Germany while the 1978 eventual winners Argentina were
beaten 1–0 by Italy.

**Is it true that Scotland were the first team to exit the
tournament undefeated?**
Yes, the Scots went out on goal difference after one win and
two draws during their 1974 group games. Belgium,
incidentally, failed to make that year's finals despite keeping
a clean sheet in their six qualifying matches.

**Which countries have hosted the World Cup on more than
one occasion?**
Mexico, Italy and France have each been awarded the
tournament twice. Mexico City's Azteca Stadium is the only
ground to have staged the final twice (in 1970 and 1986).

Which was the last country to win the tournament on its own soil?
That was Argentina who defeated Holland 3–1 in the 1978 final.

Has a country ever reached the semi-finals without having won a match from open play?
No, but the Republic of Ireland made the last eight in 1990 after three draws in the group stages and a second round penalty shoot-out victory over Romania.

Is it true that Brazil have taken part in every World Cup final tournament?
That's correct. They hadn't even lost a qualifying match until they went down 2–0 to Bolivia in La Paz in July 1993.

How many World Cup winning teams did Pelé play in?
Three, although he missed the latter stages of the 1962 tournament after being injured in a group match.

DID YOU KNOW?

⚽ In 1950, India refused to participate in the World Cup after FIFA announced that all players would have to wear boots in the finals.

⚽ One of the happiest goalscorers at the 1990 finals was Khalid Ibrahim Mubarak of the United Arab Emirates. His first round strike against West Germany earned him a Rolls-Royce.

⚽ In 1994, Cameroon State President Paul Biya cancelled all public appearances for a week after Cameroon crashed 6–1 to Russia in the World Cup.

⚽ Bookmakers William Hill made it quite clear how they felt about Diego Maradona's controversial 'Hand of God' goal of 1986. Although Argentina won the match 2–1, Hill's refunded stake money to anyone who had bet on a 1–1 scoreline.

THE EUROPEAN CHAMPIONSHIP

Germany won the European Championship for the third time in 1996. Has any other country won it more than once?
No – Spain, Italy, France, Holland, Denmark and the former Czechoslovakia and Soviet Union all have a single victory apiece.

What's England's best-ever placing?
They've reached the semi-finals twice. The first occasion was in 1968 when they lost to Yugoslavia in Florence and, of course, in 1996 they went out on penalties to Germany.

When did the competition begin?
Originally titled 'The European Nations Cup', the first tournament was held between 1958 and 1960. Several major countries, including West Germany, Italy and England, declined to enter and, in the end, only 17 of UEFA's 33 member countries took part.

Who were the first winners?
The Soviet Union lifted the Henri Delaunay trophy after a 2–1 extra-time victory over Yugoslavia in Paris. The Soviets' triumph was helped by a semi-final walk-over, awarded after Spain's Fascist leader General Franco refused to allow the national team to travel to Moscow for the first leg.

When did the tournament become known as the 'European Championship'?
The name had changed by the time the third competition

began in 1966. Italy won the 1968 final after a replay victory over Yugoslavia in Rome.

Have any other finals been replayed?
No, that was the only one. In 1976, Czechoslovakia defeated West Germany in a shoot-out after the final had finished 2–2 after extra-time. The 1996 final was decided by the 'Golden Goal' from Germany's Oliver Bierhoff.

What's the biggest upset in the final match itself?
That has to be Denmark's shock win over world champions Germany in 1992. The Danes, for whom my Rangers mate Brian Laudrup was outstanding, were the rank outsiders in Gothenburg but goals from John Jensen and Kim Vilfort gave them a sensational 2–0 victory.

Ruud Gullit captained Holland to victory in the European Championship. When was that?
That was in 1988 when the Dutch defeated the Soviet Union 2–0 in Munich. Marco van Basten's volleyed goal that day was simply out of this world!

Who holds the record for the most goals scored in a final tournament?
Between 1960 and 1976, the 'final stages' really only consisted of the semi-finals and final itself. The leading scorer in either an 8-team or 16-team tournament is Michel Platini who hit nine goals for France in 1984.

Has any player scored in the final stages of three European Championships?
Yes, German strike star Jurgen Klinsmann achieved this when he netted against Russia at Euro 96.

Who was the last player to score a hat-trick in the finals?
That was Marco van Basten, whose treble for Holland
ended England's hopes in 1988. Incidentally, van Basten's
first goal, although credited to him, has since been clearly
shown to have been an own goal by my old team-mate Gary
Stevens.

**Rangers were well-represented at Euro 96. How many of
their players took part?**
Seven. Andy Goram, Stuart McCall, Gordon Durie and myself
all played for Scotland, Gazza was in the England side while
Brian Laudrup and Erik Bo Andersen appeared for Denmark.
Incidentally, in 1992 in Sweden, seven Rangers played in the
same match – Scotland v The CIS.

**The Czech Republic and Russia drew 3–3 at Euro 96. Is
that the highest-scoring match of any finals?**
No, Yugoslavia defeated France 5–4 in the 1960 semi-final.
The Slavs had come back from 4–2 down.

**What's the biggest score in any European Championship
game?**
The most amazing result in the history of the tournament
came in the 1984 qualifying rounds. Spain needed to beat
Malta by 11 goals to qualify ahead of Holland and
(miraculously?) managed to win 12–1.

**Which country was denied that famous 'over-the-line' goal
at Euro 96?**
That was Romania, during their Group B match against
Bulgaria in Newcastle. Just about everyone inside St James'
Park was convinced that midfielder Dorinal Munteanu had
equalised when his rocket shot crashed off the bar and
down over the goal-line. However the Danish officials didn't

see it that way and the unlucky Romanians became the first
team to exit the tournament.

**What's the best performance by the other home nations in
the European Championship?**
Scotland were actually ranked fifth in the 1992 finals in
Sweden while Wales' best shot was their quarter-final
appearance in 1976. Northern Ireland have never been past
the qualifying stage although they did enjoy memorable
home-and-away victories over West Germany in the 1982–84
competition.

Where will the next European Championship be held?
Belgium and Holland will be joint-hosts for the next
tournament in the year 2000.

ENGLAND –
THE TEAM

Who's England's most-capped player?
Peter Shilton is out on his own with 125 caps won between
1970 and 1990. Shilts' total was a world record at the time.

What about outfield players?
The most-capped outfield player is Bobby Moore with 108.
He's followed by Bobby Charlton (106) and Billy Wright
(105). Wright made 70 successive appearances between
1951 and 1959 – a world record for consecutive caps.

When did England play their first-ever match?
The world's first international football game was the
meeting of Scotland and England in Partick, Glasgow in
November 1872. The match ended 0–0.

**What is the highest number of players from one club to
play in an England team?**
Seven Arsenal players represented England against world
champions Italy in November 1934. Fittingly, the match was
played at Highbury and England triumphed 3–2 with The
Gunners' Ted Drake netting the decisive goal.

**Has an Englishmen ever been the top goalscorer at the
World Cup finals?**
Yes, Gary Lineker's six goals in the 1986 finals in Mexico saw
him finish as the tournament's leading scorer.

Is Lineker England's top scorer of all time?
No, Bobby Charlton still holds that record with 49 goals, one
ahead of Gary's total of 48. Links passed up a great chance to
equal the record when he missed a penalty in one of his last
internationals, against Brazil in May 1992.

**Which teams did England defeat to win the World Cup in
1966?**
After a goal-less draw with Uruguay, England beat Mexico,
France, Argentina, Portugal and then West Germany, 4–2
after extra-time in the final.

Did any players appear in all six matches in '66?
Yes – Banks, Cohen, Wilson, Stiles, Jack Charlton, Moore,
Hunt and Bobby Charlton were all ever-presents.

**Which was the first team to beat England after they won
the World Cup?**
I'm delighted you asked that one. Scotland travelled to
Wembley in April 1967 and thrashed them 3–2.

**So which country ended England's reign as world
champions?**
That was West Germany who came back from 2–0 down to
win 3–2 in the 1970 World Cup quarter-final in Leon, Mexico.
The Germans went on to lose 4–3 to Italy in the semis.

**England lost 1–0 to Italy at Wembley in the 1998 qualifying
competition. Was that their first World Cup defeat on
home soil?**
Yes it was.

What's England's record victory?
A 13–0 demolition of Ireland in 1882. Their best post-war

scores were the 10–0 wins over Portugal in 1947 and the USA in 1964.

What about their worst-ever result?
Probably the poorest result in England's history was the 1–0 defeat by the USA in 1950, but the team's heaviest loss was a 7–1 trouncing by Hungary in Budapest in 1954.

Which player holds the record for the most goals in one match for England?
Four players have hit five, the most recent being Malcolm Macdonald against Cyprus in 1975. David Platt came close to equalling the record when he notched four in the February 1993 World Cup qualifier against San Marino and also had a penalty saved.

Matt Le Tissier was born in Guernsey. Was he the first Channel Islander to play for England?
No, Jersey-born Graeme Le Saux just pipped him to that honour. Graeme made his debut against Denmark in March 1994 while Le Tiss came on as a substitute in that game. The friendly, won 1–0 by England, was Terry Venables' first match in charge.

How many caps did Glenn Hoddle win as a player?
Glenn made 53 appearances between 1979 and 1988 and scored 8 goals, including a superb strike on his debut against Bulgaria.

Which is the most recent father-and-son combination in which both have played for England?
That's Nigel and Brian Clough who emulated George Eastham Senior and George Eastham Junior when Nigel appeared against Chile in 1989.

Who's the youngest player to have been capped by England?

James Prinsep of Clapham Rovers was only 17 years and 252 days when he made his one-and-only appearance against Scotland in 1879. The youngest cap this century is Duncan Edwards (18 years and 183 days) who was tragically killed in the 1958 Munich air crash.

Has a player from the lower divisions ever represented England?

Several have. The last was Wolves' Steve Bull who made a substitute appearance against Scotland in 1989 as a Third Division player. I played in that match at Hampden and watched from the other end as Bully hit England's second goal in their 2–0 victory.

ALLY'S TOP TEN

Ten England internationals who have played for Rangers...

Terry Butcher
Chris Woods
Graham Roberts
Ray Wilkins
Trevor Francis
Gary Stevens
Trevor Steven
Mark Hateley
Mark Walters
Paul Gascoigne

SCOTLAND –
THE TEAM

How does the Scotland-England series currently stand?
The group fixture at Euro 96 was the 107th meeting of the
countries since 1872. Scotland have won 40 of the games,
lost 43 while there have been 24 draws.

**Several Scotland stars of recent years have been born in
England. Who was the first English-born player to appear
for Scotland.**
Arsenal goalkeeper Bob Wilson, now of course well-known as
a TV presenter, was the first in 1971. Bob, whose father was
from Ayrshire, was selected under FIFA's new eligibility
regulations. Stuart McCall, incidentally, came very close to
missing out on his Scotland career. Having been selected as a
substitute for the England Under-21 side, he actually reached
the stage where he was warming up, ready to take the field.
Had he done so, he would have been ineligible for Scotland.

When did Scotland first take part in the World Cup finals?
That was in 1954 in Switzerland and a distinctly
unimpressive debut it was too. The team lost 1–0 to Austria
and then crashed 7–0 to Uruguay.

**Is it true that the Scots once took a very small squad to the
finals?**
You could say that. Only 13 players travelled to that 1954
tournament. The whole thing was apparently something of
an organisational disaster with the players having to train in
their own club jerseys.

When did Scotland first win a World Cup finals game?
Not until 1974 when they defeated Zaire 2–0 in Dortmund.
Leeds United pair Peter Lorimer and Joe Jordan were the
scorers.

**Scotland have a reputation for losing to smaller nations at
the World Cup. Is that justified?**
Partly. The defeats by Paraguay (1958), Peru (1978) and
Costa Rica (1990) were all viewed as upsets at the time.
Probably the worst performance however, was the 1–1 draw
with Iran in 1978.

What's the best World Cup goal ever scored by a Scot?
That was almost certainly Archie Gemmill's amazing solo
effort against Holland in 1978. Davie Narey's long-range
strike against Brazil in 1982, infamously described by Jimmy
Hill as a 'toe-poke', was another memorable moment.

Who is Scotland's most-capped player?
Kenny Dalglish is the only cap centurion with 102
appearances between 1971 and 1987.

**And who is the national team's leading all-time
goalscorer?**
Kenny and Denis Law share that record having scored 30
goals each.

**Alex Ferguson was Scotland manager for a while. What
was his record like?**
Fergie took over on a caretaker basis after the sad death of
Jock Stein in September 1985 and both Andy Goram and
myself have him to thank for our international debuts.
Scotland won three, lost three and drew four matches
during his nine months in charge.

Neither Craig Brown nor his predecessor Andy Roxburgh were international players themselves. Who was the last Scotland boss to have been capped?
The late Willie Ormond who was in charge from 1973 to 1977.

What was the greatest Scotland team ever?
The folklore would say the famous 'Wembley Wizards' who enjoyed a 5–1 victory over England in 1928. The Scotland side of the 1920s certainly had a great record – 24 wins and 5 draws in 34 internationals.

Have Scotland ever fielded a side without home-based players?
Yes – the eleven who started the October 1978 European Championship match against Norway were all English-based or 'Anglo-Scots'. The match was Jock Stein's first game of his 1978–85 spell and perhaps it was only the Big Man who could have got away with picking eleven Anglos!

Which club has supplied the most internationals for Scotland?
Rangers, followed by Celtic and then, perhaps surprisingly, by Queen's Park. Interestingly, the entire team for Scotland's first-ever international consisted of players who were affiliated to Queen's.

Have Scotland ever played against Rangers or Celtic?
In 1971, a Scotland XI met an Old Firm select side in a fund-raising match for the Ibrox Stadium disaster fund. Seven years later, the Scots' World Cup team crashed 5–0 to Rangers in John Greig's testimonial game.

When did Scotland's fans become known as the 'Tartan Army'?

The tag was probably first used in the 1970s at a time when Manchester United fans were calling themselves 'The Red Army' and Chelsea fans 'The Blue Army'. In 1978, comedian Andy Cameron reached No.6 in the pop charts with his record 'Ally's Tartan Army', a tribute to manager Ally MacLeod and his World Cup squad .

FOOTBALL IN EUROPE

Which mainland European club has won its domestic championship most often?
Rapid Vienna and Benfica share the honours with 30 league titles each.

Which has been Germany's most-successful club?
Bayern Munich whose 1997 championship victory was their 14th overall.

When did the Bundesliga begin?
It started in 1963. Two national first and second divisions replaced the old regional championships.

Dynamo Berlin were the top team in East Germany for a long time. Why don't we hear about them now?
During the communist era, BFC Dynamo had close associations with the despised *Stasi* (Secret Police). It was an open secret that their ten consecutive championships (1979–88) were not entirely due to their footballing ability! After the fall of the Berlin Wall, the club changed their name to FC Berlin and dropped into the obscurity of the amateur leagues.

Who are the 'Big Three' of Dutch football?
Ajax Amsterdam, PSV Eindhoven and Feyenoord of Rotterdam. Between them, they have completely dominated the Dutch championship during the past 30–40 years.

What does PSV stand for?

Philips Sport Vereniging (Philips Sports Club) – the team
have long benefited from the support of electrical giants
Philips and they are jokingly tagged the 'biggest works team
in Europe'. PSV won the UEFA Cup in 1978 and the European
Cup ten years later.

Which European league could boast the most international players during 1996–97?

Surprisingly, this was not Italy's *Serie A* or the English
Premiership but Spain's *Primera Division*.

Which has been Spain's top club?

Real Madrid and Barcelona have vied for that title since the
national championship began in 1929. Madrid have won
more honours over the years but it was the Catalans who
dominated the championship in the early 1990s.

What does 'Real' mean?

'Royal'. The team was founded in 1902, by students in
Madrid, and was granted the prefix by King Alfonso XIII in
1920. The current monarch, King Juan Carlos, is a club
member.

Barcelona have had several British players. Who were they?

Strikers Steve Archibald, Gary Lineker and Mark Hughes
have all worn the famous blue and maroon stripes. Terry
Venables, meanwhile, managed Barca to the Spanish title in
1985.

Where are Espanyol from?

RDC Espanyol are Barcelona's 'other' team. They took the
title Espanyol (meaning 'Spanish') as a reaction to the

foreign connections of FC Barcelona who had been founded
by a Swiss soccer enthusiast, Joan Gamper. Espanyol have
been nothing like as successful as their illustrious
neighbours although they did reach the UEFA Cup Final in
1988.

**Paris Saint-Germain have been successful in recent years.
Have they always been the top team in France?**
Distinctly no! PSG are actually a relatively young club,
founded in 1970 to fill the gap left by the demise of a team
called Racing Club. Amazingly, the city of Paris has the
worst record of any major European capital in terms of its
clubs winning national championships.

**Which country has teams called Young Boys and Old
Boys?**
Switzerland. Young Boys play in Berne while Old Boys hail
from Basle.

Which Greek team has fans known as 'Yellow Madness'?
AEK Athens – and a right bunch of nutters they are too! AEK
(whose full name is Athletiki Enosis Konstantinopoulos!)
knocked Rangers out of the European Cup in 1994.

Does Greek football have a hooligan problem then?
Apparently so. On one occasion, the derby between
Olympiakos (the country's most popular team) and AEK
was switched to the island of Rhodes in a bid to prevent
crowd trouble.

**Wimbledon were said to be considering a move to Dublin.
Are there any precedents in European football of a club
playing in another country's league?**
UEFA are pretty much against this unless there are strong

political reasons for it. Northern Irish club Derry City were admitted to the Republic's League of Ireland in 1985 while various Cypriot clubs regularly competed in the Greek First Division until 1975. Rapid Vienna meanwhile, can boast a unique claim to fame as the only Austrian club to have won the GERMAN league championship. They did so in 1941 at a time when Austria was part of a Greater Germany.

DID YOU KNOW?

⚽ During the days of the communist regime in East Germany, soldiers occupied the stand nearest the East-West border at Dynamo Berlin's Jahn Stadium – to prevent any potential escapes.

⚽ The holiday island of Tenerife is not a popular destination with Real Madrid. They lost both the 1991–92 and '92–93 Spanish championships there on the last day of the season.

⚽ In 1967, FC Basel won the Swiss Cup by default when their opponents Lausanne walked off the pitch.

⚽ Supporters of Crete club PAOK living in the village of Krousonas put up the club as a candidate in a 1994 election. PAOK got 70% of the votes!

THE EUROPEAN CUP

When did the European Cup begin?
The first tournament was held in the 1955–56 season and,
like the World Cup and European Championship, it was the
idea of a Frenchman, journalist Gabriel Hanot.

Which team won the first competition?
In a small field of entrants, Real Madrid overcame Servette
Geneva, Partizan Belgrade and AC Milan to reach the final in
Paris. There they defeated the French side Reims 4–3.

What's the most famous European Cup final of all time?
For many people, especially the 127,000 Scots who watched
it, that has to be the 1960 Real Madrid v Eintracht Frankfurt
match in Glasgow. Hungarian maestro Ferenc Puskas hit
four goals as Real triumphed 7–3 to lift the trophy for a fifth
consecutive time.

**So which team finally ended Madrid's domination of the
tournament?**
Ironically, it was Spanish rivals Barcelona who knocked
them out in the second round of the 1960–61 competition.
Barca went on to the final where they lost to Benfica in
Berne.

**Which country's clubs have captured the trophy on most
occasions?**
Italy's. The 1996 victory by Juventus was the ninth Italian
success in the tournament. England comes next with eight
wins followed by Spain with seven.

Has any team ever won the European Cup in their own stadium?

Yes, the last to do so was Inter Milan who defeated Benfica at the San Siro in 1965. Prior to that, Real Madrid had beaten Fiorentina in the 1957 final in Madrid. Several clubs have lifted the trophy while playing in their own country – Manchester United (1968), Ajax (1972), Liverpool (1978), Juventus (1996) and Borussia Dortmund (1997).

What is the smallest town from which the European Cup winners have come?

That's the Dutch town of Eindhoven (population 191,000), home of 1988 winners PSV.

When did the Champions League start?

It was in season 1991–92 that a league stage was introduced into the tournament for the first time. Sampdoria and Barcelona reached the final after winning their respective four-team semi-final groups. The following season, the group stage was renamed the Champions League.

The tournament was extended in 1997 to include the league runners-up from the top eight UEFA countries. Was that the first time that non-champions, apart from the holders, have taken part in the competition?

No, in actual fact it's not. For the inaugural tournament in 1955–56, UEFA invited several famous teams who didn't hold their national title. For example, Hibs were Britain's first-ever representatives although Aberdeen were the champions of Scotland at the time.

Since Borussia Dortmund were the holders, Germany entered three teams in the 1997–98 Champions League. Would it be possible for a team finishing third in its national league to gain entry?

No, UEFA have stipulated that a team finishing third in its domestic league will never be invited, unless of course they are the holders.

Has any club ever fielded a full team of non-nationals in a European Cup final?

Not quite – although in 1985, ELEVEN non-English nationals appeared for Liverpool at some stage of the final against Juventus.

Which was the last team to win the final with only home-grown players?

Steaua Bucharest in 1986. You have to say that seems unlikely to happen again in the post-Bosman era.

Since the Champions League began, has any team ever defeated the same opponents three times during the course of one tournament?

Ajax became the first to do this when they triumphed 1–0 against AC Milan in the 1995 final having already defeated the Italians home and away in the group stages.

Has any club won the European Cup more often than its own national championship?

Yes – Nottingham Forest lifted the trophy in 1979 and 1980 but have just one English League title (in 1978) to their name.

It seems to be that one goal has often been enough to win the Champions League final. How many finals have ended with that scoreline?

In the 42 Champions' Cup finals contested between 1956 and 1997, 14 ended 1–0. However, 1–0 has been the result in 11 of the last 20 finals.

Have two teams from the same city ever met in the Champions' Cup?

Real Madrid and Atletico Madrid played three derby matches in the 1959 semi-finals. Real eventually won after a play-off in Zaragoza.

THE CUP-WINNERS' CUP

When was the European Cup-Winners' Cup first contested?
The first Cup-Winners' Cup competition was held in 1960–61, making it the youngest of the three European tournaments. Fiorentina defeated Rangers in the one and only two-legged final.

How many clubs entered the first tournament?
Only ten. At the time, there were relatively few national cup competitions of the sort held in England and Scotland. In fact, several countries either revived their cup tournaments or created new ones solely to provide one of their clubs with the experience of European competition.

Which team has won the Cup-Winners' Cup most often?
Barcelona, who have lifted the trophy on four occasions – (1979, 1982, 1989 and 1997). Barca's 1997 final victory over Paris Saint-Germain gave them their eighth European tournament success overall, equalling the record held by rivals Real Madrid.

Is it right that PSG were bidding to be the first team to retain the trophy?
Yes, for some reason there have been numerous occasions in which the holders have lost in the final. This happened to Fiorentina (1962), Atletico Madrid (1963), AC Milan (1974), Anderlecht (1977), Ajax (1988), Parma (1994), Arsenal (1995) and PSG (1997).

The 1997 final was held in Rotterdam. Has that been the most popular location for the final?
The Feyenoord Stadium has now hosted six finals, followed by Basle and Brussels with four each.

Who was the Real Zaragoza player who hit that amazing winning goal against Arsenal in 1995?
That was Mohamed Ali Amar, better known as 'Nayim', whose outrageous 45-yard lob in the last minute of extra-time was one of the most sensational goals ever scored in a European final. I'm sure big Dave Seaman is still having nightmares about it!

Has one city ever been represented in both the Champions' Cup and Cup-Winners' Cup finals in the same season?
That's happened on three occasions – 1962 (Real and Atletico Madrid), 1967 (Celtic and Rangers) and 1985 (Liverpool and Everton). Only Atletico, Celtic and Everton won their finals however.

Alex Ferguson won the European Cup-Winners' Cup with both Aberdeen and Manchester United. Has any other manager steered two different clubs to the trophy?
Johan Cruyff did so with Ajax in 1987 and Barcelona in 1989.

No team from the former East Germany ever won the Champions' Cup. Did they fare any better in the Cup-Winners' tournament?
Yes they did. FC Magdeburg lifted the trophy by defeating AC Milan in 1974 while Carl Zeiss Jena (1981) and Lokomotiv Leipzig (1987) were both runners-up.

What's the biggest score in a Cup-Winners' Cup final?
The best final victories were Tottenham's 5–1 defeat of
Atletico Madrid in 1963 and Anderlecht's 4–0 triumph
against Austria Vienna in 1978. Jimmy Greaves netted twice
for Spurs in '63.

What's the record victory in a single match?
That was 16–1 by Sporting Lisbon against Apoel Nicosia
in 1963–64. The biggest aggregate win was Chelsea's 21–0
triumph over Luxembourg side Jeunesse Hautcharage
in 1971.

**Which player holds the record for most goals in a Cup-
Winners' Cup tournament?**
Borussia Dortmund's Lothar Emmerich set an individual
scoring record for the competition with 14 goals during his
club's successful campaign of 1965–66.

Has a second division side ever won the trophy?
No, although Atalanta came close in 1988. The Bergamo-
based side were a *Serie B* outfit when they lost to KV
Mechelen in the Cup-Winners' Cup semi-finals.

Has any team ever appeared in three consecutive finals?
Anderlecht did just that between 1976 and 1978, winning
two of the three games.

**Is it true that West Ham once played against a reserve
team in the Cup-Winners' Cup tournament?**
In a manner of speaking, yes. In 1980, Real Madrid defeated
their own nursery side, Castilla CF, in the Spanish Cup final
and since Real had also won the championship, Castilla
went on to represent Spain in the Cup-Winners' Cup. West
Ham beat them 6–4 on aggregate in the first round.

**Has any team ever won the European Cup-Winners' Cup
without being the holders of their own national cup?**
Rangers became the first club to do this in 1972. The Gers
had qualified for the tournament after losing the Scottish
Cup final to League champions Celtic.

THE UEFA CUP

The UEFA Cup was previously known by a different name. What was it?
The tournament began life under the snappy title of 'The International Inter-City Industrial Fairs Cup' and it was originally set up as a competition between cities rather than clubs.

Who won the inaugural tournament?
The first competition, which spanned almost three years between 1955 and 1958, was won by Barcelona who defeated a composite London select 8–2 on aggregate in the final. Two years later, Barca retained the trophy by defeating Birmingham City who had become the first British club side to appear in a European final.

From 1998 onwards, the UEFA Cup final will be played as a single leg tie. Has the competition ever used that format before?
Yes, twice during the Fairs Cup era. In 1964, Real Zaragoza defeated Valencia in an all-Spanish affair in Barcelona while, the following season, Ferencvaros travelled to Turin and notched a surprise victory over a Juventus team who were playing on their own patch.

Which country has enjoyed the most success in the tournament?
Spain dominated the early years of the Fairs Cup with six triumphs in the first eight competitions but English clubs enjoyed a good run of success in the late '60s and early '70s. In recent seasons, Italian clubs have had the upper hand but

England still lead overall with nine victories to Italy and Spain's eight apiece.

So when did the competition become the UEFA Cup?

The tournament was renamed in 1971 and Tottenham became the first holders of the new trophy after defeating Wolves in an all-English final.

What happened to the old Fairs Cup trophy?

Barcelona, the original and three-times winners met Leeds United, the last winners in 1971, in a one-off match to decide the permanent home of the trophy. Barca, with home advantage, defeated Don Revie's team 2–1.

Did any player score in both a Fairs Cup and UEFA Cup final?

As a youngster, Ray Kennedy scored a crucial goal for Arsenal in the 1970 Fairs Cup final and was on target again six years later, during Liverpool's UEFA Cup triumph over Club Bruges.

Has any country ever completely dominated one season's competition?

In 1980, all four semi-finalists were German clubs – Bayern Munich, Eintracht Frankfurt, VfB Stuttgart and Borussia Monchengladbach. Eintracht defeated Monchengladbach on the away goals rule in the final.

What's the best comeback in the final?

That has to be the performance of Bayer Leverkusen who turned round a three-goal deficit in 1988. The Germans, having crashed 3–0 to Espanyol in the first leg, won the return by the same score and went on to take the Cup on a penalty shoot-out.

Who was the first player to win medals from all three European tournaments?

When he helped AC Milan to victory in the 1969 Champions' Cup final, goalkeeper Fabio Cudicini became the first player to appear on the winning side in all three European tournament finals. He had won a Fairs Cup medal with AS Roma in 1961 and a Cup-Winners' Cup badge with Milan in '68.

How many clubs have won all three European competitions?

Four – Juventus, Barcelona, Ajax and Bayern Munich.

Has any team ever lifted the UEFA Cup by winning all their matches?

No, but Bayern Munich completed an unprecedented clean sweep of six away victories during their successful run of 1995–96.

Jurgen Klinsmann hit a barrowload of goals during Bayern's run that season. How many did he score?

Klinsi banged in 15 in total – a record haul in a single European campaign. My fellow Scotsman John Wark had earlier notched 14 goals during Ipswich Town's victorious season of 1980–81.

What's the best individual scoring performance in a single UEFA Cup match?

The 'White Feather' Fabrizio Ravanelli made history by scoring all five goals for Juventus in their 5–1 win against CSKA Sofia in a 1994–95 first round second leg game.

When did the 'away goals' rule come into being?

The rule was introduced by UEFA in 1965 to help settle

deadlocked ties in the Cup-Winners' Cup. Dinamo Zagreb became the first team to benefit in a Fairs Cup context when they eliminated Dunfermline Athletic in the second round of the 1966–67 tournament.

What's the greatest number of matches played by one team during a single season of European competition?
The 1995–96 UEFA Cup runners-up Bordeaux contested an amazing total of 20 European games during that season. The French side had qualified for the UEFA Cup via the previous summer's InterToto Cup tournament.

FOOTBALL ITALIA

Which is Italy's most-popular club?
According to a recent survey, Juventus, nicknamed 'The Old Lady', are the best supported club in the *Serie A* with around seven million fans, two million of whom reside in southern Italy.

Juventus are based in the northern city of Turin – why do so many southern Italians support them?
Juventus have attracted many of the South's top players over the years. This meant that the migrant workers, who moved to Turin from the likes of Sicily and Puglia, felt a bond with the team.

What about Turin's other club, Torino. Have they ever been front-runners?
The *Granata* (Clarets) were the leading Italian side of the 1940s. In May 1949, they were on the verge of a fifth consecutive championship when the club was struck by a desperate tragedy. All of their players were killed in an air crash at Superga on the hills above Turin.

Why are Inter Milan so-called?
Inter is short for Internazionale. The club was founded in 1908 by Italian and Swiss players who apparently resented the dominant British influence at Milan FC.

What is the *Scudetto*?
The *Scudetto* is the red, white and green shield worn by the champions on their shirts.

Why do Juventus wear two gold stars on their strip?
Each star represents ten championship victories. Both AC
Milan and Inter carry one star on their jerseys.

Which of the Milan giants has won the more trophies?
Their successes during the past decade have seen AC Milan
overtake Inter in terms of both domestic and European
honours.

Who was the first British-born player to play in Italy?
That was Giovanni 'Johnny' Moscardini, a Scottish-Italian
from Falkirk who had joined the Italian army during World
War One. After the war Johnny played for Lucchese and
went on to win nine caps for Italy.

**Who has been the most successful British player in Italian
football?**
That's open to debate but there is a very strong case for
big John Charles, the Welshman signed by Juventus from
Leeds in 1957. Nicknamed 'The Gentle Giant', Charles
netted 93 league goals during his five seasons in Turin – a
club record.

**Why did Italy ban the importing of foreign players
between 1964 and 1978?**
The authorities were concerned about the national team's
poor showing in the 1962 World Cup and their failure to
qualify for the 1958 tournament.

What effect did the ban have?
Both a positive and a negative one. On one hand, a new
generation of native Italian players emerged which
ultimately led to the World Cup triumph of 1982. However,
by the 1970s, the big Italian sides were missing their foreign

stars and went through a relatively lean period in European competition.

Who were the top foreign players during the 1980s?

Probably the most influential *stranieri* (foreigners) were Michel Platini, a double championship winner with Juventus, and Diego Maradona who almost single-handedly put Napoli back on the footballing map. In the later '80s, Milan's three Dutchmen (Gullit, Rijkaard and Van Basten) provided the backbone of their outstanding side while the German duo of Brehme and Matthaus helped Inter win the *Scudetto* in 1989.

Which is Rome's oldest club – Roma or Lazio?

Taking their name from the region around the city, Lazio were formed in 1900 and pre-date AS (*Associazione Sportiva*) Roma by 27 years. Lazio tend to draw their support from the suburbs as opposed to the more city-centre based Roma following.

What is *Il Derby del Sud* (The Derby of the South)?

That's the tag given to the match between Roma and Napoli, often a heated affair.

When did a provincial club last win the *Serie A*?

1985, when Verona took the title by four points from Torino.

Who is Italy's most capped player of all time?

That's Dino Zoff, the goalkeeper who made 112 appearances between 1968 and 1983. Zoff also captained their World Cup winning side of '82.

Roberto Baggio must have scored a lot of goals for the national team. Is he their top scorer?
No, the 'Divine Ponytail' had netted 25 times for the *Azzurri* by the end of 1996–97 but he's still well behind Luigi Riva, the explosive Cagliari striker who bagged 35 goals between 1965 and 1974.

ALLY'S TOP TEN

Ten famous Scottish victories against Italian teams…

Celtic 2 Inter Milan 1 (1967)
Hibs 5 Napoli 0 (1967)
Celtic 3 Fiorentina 0 (1970)
Dundee 2 AC Milan 0 (1971)
Rangers 1 Torino 0 (1972)
Rangers 2 Juventus 0 (1978)
Celtic 1 Juventus 0 (1981)
Dundee United 2 Roma 0 (1984)
Rangers 3 Inter Milan 1 (1984)
Hearts 3 Bologna 1 (1990)

BRITS IN EUROPE

Which was the first British side to play in European competition?
That was Hibs in the 1955–56 Champions' Cup. They defeated Rot-Weiss Essen and Djurgardens of Stockholm before losing to Reims in the semi-final.

What about English clubs?
Chelsea were invited to enter the first Champions' Cup tournament but declined after the Football League advised against it. Manchester United took part in 1956–57 and reached the semi-finals.

When did a British team first win a European trophy?
That came in 1963 when Spurs defeated Atletico Madrid in the Cup-Winners' Cup final. The Londoners knocked out Rangers en route.

How many trophies has Britain won altogether?
British clubs have enjoyed 27 European competition victories overall (nine in each of the tournaments).

Which Scottish clubs have won European trophies?
Rangers (1972) and Aberdeen (1983) have both lifted the Cup-Winners' Cup while Celtic, in 1967, were the first British team to win the Champions' Cup. Aberdeen also captured the European Super Cup in 1983 by defeating European champions Hamburg.

Has any British side appeared in all three European club tournament finals?

Leeds and Liverpool have. Unfortunately Leeds lost in both the Champions' Cup and Cup-Winners' Cup finals while Liverpool were beaten by Borussia Dortmund in their Cup-Winners' Cup final appearance in 1966.

Who's the top British goalscorer in European competition?

Former Scottish international Peter Lorimer who hit 31 goals in nine European campaigns with Leeds.

Manchester United lost at home to Juventus in the 1996–97 Champions League. Was that their first defeat in a European match at Old Trafford?

No, that came three weeks earlier when a goal from Bosnian Elvir Bolic gave Turkish side Fenerbahce a shock 1–0 win over the English champions. It was in fact United's first home loss in over 40 years of European competition.

Which British club has appeared most often in European competition?

Rangers have played more seasons (37 including 1997–98) in European competition than any other British club. Liverpool are England's top representatives while Glentoran have flown Northern Ireland's flag on most occasions.

Swindon won the League Cup in 1969 but there's no record of them playing in Europe. Why is that?

Swindon were prohibited from entering the Fairs Cup simply because they were a lower division side.

Has Britain ever been represented in all three European finals in a single season?
In 1970, Celtic, Manchester City and Arsenal played in the Champions' Cup, Cup-Winners' Cup and Fairs Cup finals respectively.

Which was the first British team to take part in the Champions League?
Rangers claimed that distinction in 1992–93. We were actually undefeated in the six matches although Marseille just pipped us for a final spot.

The 1992–93 European Cup saw a famous 'Battle of Britain' clash between Rangers and Leeds. Was that the first time that Scottish and English clubs had met in the tournament?
I have to say that night at Leeds was absolutely fantastic and one of the happiest moments of my life. It was actually the third such meeting in the competition – Celtic beat Leeds home and away in 1970 and Liverpool did the same to Aberdeen ten years later.

Why was the 1992 Leeds v Stuttgart tie replayed?
The Germans had breached UEFA regulations by fielding four foreign players during the second leg at Elland Road.

Has an Englishman ever played against a British team in a Champions' Cup Final?
Kevin Keegan was in the Hamburg side which lost to Nottingham Forest in 1980 while Laurie Cunningham turned out for Real Madrid against Liverpool the following year.

What's the most semi-finalists Britain has had in a single European season?
I make it six, in both 1965–66 and 1983–84. In 1983–84, the clubs were Liverpool, Dundee United, Manchester United, Aberdeen, Tottenham and Nottingham Forest. Liverpool and Spurs made it through to their respective finals.

How long were English clubs banned from Europe?
For five years, between 1985 and 1990.

Did Gary Lineker ever win a European tournament medal?
Yes, Gary was in the Barcelona side which defeated Sampdoria to lift the Cup-Winners' Cup in 1989.

What is the best performance by a Welsh club in Europe?
Cardiff City reached the semi-finals of the Cup-Winners' Cup in 1968 but arguably the best single result achieved was Bangor City's stunning 2–0 first leg victory over Napoli in the same tournament in 1962. In 1993, Cwmbran Town made history by becoming the first Welsh club to compete in the Champions' Cup.

GOALKEEPERS

Did teams always play with a goalkeeper?
They were first mentioned in the Laws of the Game in 1871.
Interestingly, it wasn't until 1912 that 'keepers were banned
from handling outside the penalty area.

**Is it true that England once had a goalkeeper who weighed
20 stone?**
Amazingly, yes. William 'Fatty' Foulke was his name and he
is reputed to have tipped the scales somewhere between 22
and 26 stone! He played around the turn of the century and
helped Sheffield United to League Championship and FA
Cup victory.

Is Andy Goram Scotland's most-capped goalkeeper?
No, he's not. Jim Leighton has also been a superb 'keeper for
the national team and he won his 82nd cap against Belarus
in September 1997.

**Chris Woods created some sort of new goalkeeping record
while with Rangers. What was it?**
During season 1986–87, Woodsie went for a British-record of
1,196 minutes without conceding a goal.

So what's the world record for a clean sheet?
It stands at 1,275 minutes and was set during 1990–91 by
Atletico Madrid goalkeeper Abel Resino. The record for
international matches is held by Italy's Dino Zoff who
completed 1,142 minutes of shut-out between September
1972 and June 1974.

What's the most outstanding performance by a 'keeper in a match in Britain?

Difficult to say, but certainly the BRAVEST display came from Bert Trautmann, the German who starred in Manchester City's FA Cup final victory of 1956. Trautmann played out the closing minutes of the match with a broken neck, sustained after a sickening collision with a Birmingham forward.

Who was the 'Clown of Wembley'?

That was Jan Tomaszewski who, in October 1973, turned in a brilliant performance to help Poland draw at Wembley and oust England from the World Cup. Before the game, TV pundit Brian Clough had maintained that the Polish No.1 was 'a clown'.

Who's been the most successful goalkeeper in the World Cup tournament?

In terms of medals won, the Brazilian Gylmar is the only 'keeper to have played in two World Cup winning teams (1958 and 1962).

Have any goalkeepers ever captained England?

Yes. Alexander Morton was the first in 1873 and there have been five others including Ray Clemence and Peter Shilton. Shilts is the only England 'keeper to have lifted a trophy as skipper – he collected the Rous Cup after England's 1986 win over Scotland.

Several goalkeepers have been on the scoresheet themselves. What's the most famous goal by a 'keeper?

There have been quite a few instances of long clearances ending in the net, most notably the one from Tottenham's Pat Jennings in the 1967 Charity Shield match against

Manchester United. In September 1995, Peter Schmeichel's headed equaliser for Manchester United against Rotor Volgograd in a UEFA Cup tie even made the headlines on *News at Ten*!

Who's the South American goalie who comes upfield to take free-kicks and penalties?
That's Jose Luis Chilavert, the Paraguayan who's netted well over 30 goals and is way out in front as the highest-scoring goalkeeper in modern football.

Has any goalkeeper ever netted a hat-trick?
I know of one definite case. Radnicki Nis 'keeper Dragon Pantelic converted three penalties in a Yugoslavian League match against NK Zagreb during the 1980–81 season.

What's the biggest goalkeeping blunder of all time?
As you can imagine there have been a few, but I like the one attributed to Lord Kinnaird in the 1877 FA Cup Final between Wanderers and Oxford University. It's said that he shouted for the ball, caught it, then stepped backwards over his own goal-line!

Before Jim Leighton and Andy Goram, Scottish goalkeepers had something of a bad reputation, did they not?
They did. Certainly a couple of our 'keepers have turned in nightmare displays in high-profile England-Scotland matches at Wembley, most notoriously Frank Haffey in 1961 and Stewart Kennedy in 1975.

I heard something recently about Chesterfield being famous for goalkeepers. Why is that?
The Derbyshire town is the birthplace of top goalkeeping

expert Bob Wilson and double championship medallist John Lukic. Chesterfield FC, meanwhile, was the first club of Premiership veteran Steve Ogrizovic and England's legendary World Cup winning 'keeper Gordon Banks.

Quite a few famous people have at one time been goalkeepers. Can you name some of them?
Right, here goes: David Icke (ex-Hereford and Coventry City, snooker commentator and occasional Son of God), Julio Iglesias (singer), Pope John Paul II and Albert Camus (well-known French-Algerian existentialist philosopher).

THE NAME GAME

Why are Rangers and Celtic collectively known as the 'Old Firm'?
The tag dates back to the early years of this century when the two teams began to dominate Scottish football. The nickname referred both to the frequency of their meetings and the commercial rewards which their rivalry generated.

Why Sheffield 'Wednesday'?
The club are descended from the Sheffield Wednesday Cricket Club which was so-called because the players met on Wednesday half-day holidays. They take their nickname 'The Owls' from Owlerton, the original name of the district in which their ground is situated.

Are there any other teams named after days of the week?
There's a Welsh club called Abergavenny Thursdays. Incidentally, you may also have heard of Nigerian players called Friday Eduho and Sunday Oliseh.

Why are Port Vale so-called?
Vale are named after the house where the founders met to form the club. They formerly used the prefix 'Burslem' after the area of Stoke in which they play.

What's the origin of the team name 'Albion'?
Albion was an ancient name for Britain.

Why are West Bromwich Albion nicknamed 'The Baggies'?
One theory is that it's a throwback to the days when most of

Albion's fans were ironworkers. They would work in the morning then go straight to the match in their baggy, oversize workclothes, giving rise to the nickname. Interestingly, when West Brom toured China in 1978, the Chinese translated the nickname as 'the team who plays in very wide trousers!'

Why are Aberdeen known as 'The Dons'?
According to the club history, the most likely explanation is that it's a simple contraction of 'Aberdonian', turning initially into 'Come on the 'Donians' and then to 'Come on the Dons'.

Which English League clubs have the longest and shortest names?
That would be Wolverhampton Wanderers and Bury respectively.

What's the most common name for an English League club?
'United' and 'City' share the honours. There were 15 of each in 1997–98.

What about in Scotland?
'Athletic' shades it as the most popular team name in Scotland, although there are only three of them – Dunfermline, Forfar and Alloa.

What's the most famous player nickname?
Arguably it's the 'Wizard of Dribble' label given to the legendary Blackpool, Stoke and England winger Stanley Matthews. Incidentally, Sir Stan once made a guest appearance for Rangers in a wartime league match against Morton in March 1940.

Is it true that 'Pelé' was merely a nickname?
Yes. The famous Brazilian's real name is Edson Arantes do
Nascimento and it was a boy at his school who gave him the
tag 'Pelé'. Originally, he wasn't too keen on the name but it
stuck before he could do much about it.

So are most Brazilian stars known by their nicknames?
Indeed, and you can understand why when you hear their
real names. For instance, Zico was Artur Antunes Coimbra
while the full name of Pelé's 1970 team-mate Tostao was
Eduardo Goncalves de Andrade!

**Why are so many Eastern European teams called
'Dynamo'?**
It originally suggested a link with workers in the power
industries.

**What is the correct name of that famous Croatian team – is
it Hadjuk Split or Hajduk Split?**
It's definitely Hajduk (pronounced 'High-dook') and they are
called after the local bandits who fought against the Turkish
Ottoman occupation.

What is the '04' in the name of Schalke 04?
It represents the year of formation – 1904. The
Gelsenkirchen side, UEFA Cup winners in 1997, have
traditionally been one of Germany's most popular teams.

**Xamax Neuchatel seems an unusual name for a team.
What's the story behind that?**
The club are called after a founding member, Swiss
international Max 'Xam' Abegglen.

Is it true that there was once a Premiership referee from a place called Great Bookham?
That was Ray Lewis and, appropriately enough, he yellow carded 52 players during 1992–93!

ALLY'S TOP TEN

Ten former names of league clubs…

Ardwick FC (Manchester City)
Black Arabs (Bristol Rovers)
Dial Square FC (Arsenal)
Dundee Hibernians (Dundee United)
Leicester Fosse (Leicester City)
Newton Heath LYR (Manchester United)
Pine Villa (Oldham)
St Mary's YMCA (Southampton)
Thames Ironworks (West Ham)
Wee Alpha (Motherwell)

STADIA

Which stadium housed the world's biggest-ever football crowd?
That was the Maracana in Rio de Janeiro where an incredible 199,850 people gathered to watch Brazil play Uruguay in the deciding match of the 1950 World Cup finals.

Which ground holds the attendance record for a league match in Britain?
Ibrox can claim that distinction – a crowd of 118,567 saw the Old Firm game of January 1939. In England, the top League attendance is the 83,260 for the 1948 Manchester United v Arsenal fixture at Maine Road.

Why were Manchester United playing at City's ground, Maine Road?
Old Trafford had been badly damaged by a German bomb during World War Two. United finally returned home in 1949 after an eight-year absence.

Has Ibrox ever hosted a European competition final?
No, apart from Rangers' home leg of the 1961 Cup-Winners' Cup final against Fiorentina. The Stadium did appear set to stage the 1996 Cup-Winners' Cup final until a convention of cardiologists threw a spanner in the works. The heart docs booked up all Glasgow's top hotel rooms around the time of the game and forced UEFA to switch the match to Brussels.

Why is Aberdeen's Pittodrie Stadium so-called?
Apparently, the name can be translated from Celtic as 'place

of manure' – quite appropriate since the ground is situated on the former site of a dung heap.

How did Liverpool's famous Kop acquire its name?

The tag comes originally from 'Spion Kop', a hill on which many Liverpudlian soldiers fought and died during the Boer War. The name (which means 'look-out' in Afrikaans) was also adopted by several other clubs who called their high-banking terraces after the hill.

Which was the first football ground to have floodlights?

In 1878, Sheffield United's Bramall Lane became the first venue anywhere in the world to stage a football match under lights. Of the present League clubs, Oxford United were the first to install floodlights as we know them.

When did floodlighting become the norm for midweek games?

The Football Association actually had a ban on lights until 1950 but, by the middle of the decade, the era of floodlit football had definitely arrived. Clubs like Wolves had shown its potential with lucrative friendlies against European opponents. Rangers staged the first-ever official floodlit Scottish League match when they defeated Queen of the South 8–0 in March 1956.

Which English club has had the most grounds since its formation?

That's Queens Park Rangers who have had twelve grounds in total and have also played home matches at two other venues.

Didn't QPR have an artificial pitch at one time. What happened to it?

QPR played on their 'Omniturf' surface for seven seasons between 1981 and 1988. The idea fell out of favour with the football authorities who instructed all clubs to return to grass.

Apart from the play-off finals, has Wembley ever staged a Football League match?
Yes, Clapton Orient played two Third Division games there in 1930 while their own ground was out of commission.

Has any person attended matches at all 92 English League grounds during a single season?
This rather exhausting feat was first completed during 1968–69 and has been repeated several times since.

Which British ground is closest to the sea?
That's Arbroath's Gayfield Park. Shrewsbury's Gay Meadow, situated on the banks of the River Severn, is the nearest to water however.

Where are the world's closest football grounds?
Budapest can claim that honour – the grounds of MTK and BKV Elore are situated back-to-back and separated only by a narrow roadway. The closest stadia in Britain are Dundee's Dens Park and Dundee United's Tannadice which are only 100 yards apart.

When Stockholm's Rasunda Stadium is on the TV, the stand always looks full even when the ends are empty. Why is that?
A cunning use of randomly-placed blue, orange and red seats gives the effect that the stand is full whether there's a crowd there or not!

How many different stadia will be used for the 1998 World Cup finals?

Ten in all, many of which are being revamped specially for the tournament. For example, Marseille's Velodrome where we played with Rangers in 1993, will have its capacity increased from 46,000 to 60,000.

Which stadium will host the final?

The final will be held in the specially-constructed Stade de France in Saint-Denis, near Paris. The four-tiered, elliptical ground has a capacity of 80,000.

TRANSFERS

Who was the first player to move for £1,000?
That was Alf Common who was bought by Middlesbrough
from Sunderland in February 1905.

When were the £10,000 and £50,000 barriers broken?
Bolton's David Jack joined Arsenal for £10,000 in 1928 while
Welsh international John Charles moved from Leeds to
Juventus for a then-princely sum of £65,000 in 1957.

**Why did Tottenham pay AC Milan exactly £99,999 for
Jimmy Greaves in 1962?**
The fee was set at that amount because Spurs claimed that
they didn't want to saddle Greavsie with the pressure of
Britain's first six-figure transfer – and probably also because
they themselves didn't want to be the first club to pay such
an 'inflationary' price. Denis Law had earlier become the
first Briton to move for £100,000 when he joined Torino from
Manchester City in 1961.

Who was the world's first £1 million footballer?
That honour goes to Giuseppe Savoldi who switched from
Bologna to Napoli for what must have been a lorry-load of
lira in July 1975. In Britain, my old Rangers team-mate
Trevor Francis broke the £1 million barrier when
Nottingham Forest signed him from Birmingham in
February 1979.

What has been the most controversial transfer of all time?
Most Old Firm fans would say Rangers' signing of ex-Celtic
star Maurice Johnston in 1989. On his return from French

football, wee Mo had looked set to rejoin his old club when
Graeme Souness swooped to bring him to Ibrox.

How much profit did Blackburn Rovers make when they sold Alan Shearer to Newcastle in 1996?

Rovers bought the England star for £3.3 million in July 1992
and sold him on for a cool £15 million four years later. By my
arithmetic that makes a healthy profit of £11.7 million!

Who was the first British goalkeeper to be transferred for £1 million?

Nigel Martyn, who moved from Bristol Rovers to Crystal
Palace in November 1989.

Has any £1 million signing ever been handed a free transfer?

Several have, but the first was the late Laurie Cunningham
who was released by Real Madrid in 1984, five years after
they had paid West Bromwich Albion a seven-figure sum for
him.

How many different London clubs has Clive Allen played for?

Seven – QPR, Arsenal, Crystal Palace, Tottenham, Chelsea,
West Ham and Millwall. In actual fact, it's eight – if you count
the London Monarchs American Football team!

David Platt has been the subject of several big money moves during his career. How much has been spent on his transfers?

Since 1988, somewhere in the region of £22 million has
changed hands for Platty. At the end of 1996–97, that was a
world record amount for one player.

How did the Bosman ruling affect transfers?
The judgement, made by the European Court in December 1995, outlawed the imposition of transfer fees for footballers who were out of contract and who wanted to move to another EC member state.

Who was Bosman exactly?
Jean-Marc Bosman was a little-known Belgian player who became aggrieved in 1990 when RFC Liege, the club with whom his contract had just ended, blocked his transfer to French side US Dunkerque. Bosman started legal proceedings which eventually culminated in the historic ruling five years later.

When is the transfer Deadline Day?
It's the fourth Thursday in March during each season. Any transfers taking place after that may be declined or, even if they are allowed, the players will usually only be permitted to appear in matches which have no bearing on promotion or relegation.

What's the closest any move has come to missing the transfer deadline?
On the 1967 deadline day of 16 March, the transfer of Bill Atkins from Halifax Town to Stockport County was completed at four seconds before midnight. Phew!

Who has been the most successful British export abroad?
Kevin Keegan must have a good claim for that honour. He helped Hamburg win the Bundesliga title, learned to speak German and even managed a hit single in the German pop charts!

What's the strangest transfer fee ever paid?
Legend has it that former Republic of Ireland and Celtic
striker Tony Cascarino was transferred from Crockenhill to
Gillingham for a set of tracksuits and a piece of corrugated
iron! Meanwhile, Daniel Allende's 1979 move between
Uruguayan clubs Central Espanol and Rentistas was based
on a particularly tasty transfer fee – 550 beef steaks!

ALLY'S TOP TEN

Ten £1 million Rangers signings…

Richard Gough (£1.5m from Tottenham, Oct 1987)
Gary Stevens (£1m from Everton, Jul 1988)
Trevor Steven (£1.5m from Everton, Jun 1989)
Oleg Kuznetsov (£1.2m from Dynamo Kiev, Sep 1990)
Alexei Mikhailitchenko (£2.2m from Sampdoria, Jul 1991)
Dave McPherson (£1.3m from Hearts, Jun 1992)
Duncan Ferguson (£4m from Dundee United, Jul 1993)
Brian Laudrup (£2.2m from Fiorentina, Jul 1994)
Paul Gascoigne (£4.3m from Lazio, Jul 1995)
Joachim Bjorklund (£2.6m from Vicenza, Jul 96)

DERBY DAYS

What's the origin of the term 'derby match'?
It seems to have come from a traditional Shrovetide game
which was fiercely contested between two rival parishes in
the town of Derby.

What is the world's biggest derby game?
That's a very debatable point – fans in Glasgow, Liverpool,
Milan and Rome all might stake a claim for their city.
However, the Rio derby between Flamengo and Fluminense
holds the world attendance record for a club match –
177,656 saw them clash in 1963.

**Which team has had the upper hand in Liverpool v
Everton games?**
The answer is neither really. In the 156 League games played
to the end of 1996–97, Liverpool won 56, Everton 52 and
there were been 48 draws.

How many times have the teams met in major cup finals?
Three times, with Liverpool winning on each occasion – the
1984 Milk Cup final (after a replay) and the FA Cup finals of
1986 and 1989.

**Peter Beardsley played and scored for both clubs in
Merseyside derbies. Was he the first player to do so?**
No, 1970s striker David Johnson was the first.

**What about the Manchester derby – has either team
dominated that?**
The results are slightly tipped in favour of United who have
won 48 League matches to City's 32.

Have United and City ever met at Wembley?
No. United defeated their rivals 1–0 in the 1956 Charity
Shield match but that was played at Maine Road.

**United trounced City 5–0 a couple of seasons back. Was
that their biggest-ever derby win?**
Yes, the November 1994 match, in which Andrei Kanchelskis
hit a hat-trick, was indeed their finest result in the fixture.
City's top victory was 6–1 in January 1926.

How do the Rangers v Celtic standings look?
Of the 244 League matches played by the end of the 1996–97
season, Rangers had won 97, Celtic 74 with 73 ending in
draws. In the 88 Premier League fixtures between 1975–76
and 1996–97, the Gers won 31 to Celtic's 30 with 27 draws.

**Did Maurice Johnston score for both teams in Old Firm
games?**
Yes he did. He netted two League and one Glasgow Cup goal
for Celtic and three League goals for Rangers. Mo was so
chuffed with his November 1989 winner against his old club
that he was booked for over-celebrating!

Do Rangers and Celtic always meet at New Year?
They've done so since the 1890s. There was a period
however when it was decided that the teams wouldn't face
each other on 1 January itself. Between 1967 and 1975, the
Gers usually met Partick Thistle on New Year's Day while
Celtic played Clyde.

**Hearts have dominated the Edinburgh derby in recent
years. How many consecutive matches did they go
undefeated?**
Hearts were unbeaten in 22 matches with Hibs between
April 1989 and August 1994.

What British city derby has been played the least frequently?
Although they are fierce rivals, neighbours Stoke and Port Vale have met on relatively few occasions – only 38 league matches in all (at the end of 1996–97). That's because Stoke have usually been in a higher division than Vale.

Can you think of any ex-Rangers players who have appeared in other major derbies?
Andy Gray played in derby matches in Dundee, Birmingham and Liverpool while Ray Wilkins ('Razor' to us) has featured in Milan, Edinburgh, Manchester and numerous London derbies.

How many FA Cup finals have been London derbies?
Surprisingly, there have been only four since the final moved to Wembley in 1923. The first was Chelsea v Tottenham in 1967, then West Ham defeated Fulham (1975) and Arsenal (1980) before Tottenham and QPR clashed in 1982.

Does German football have any big derby matches?
There are several. City derbies include Bayern v 1860 Munich and Hamburg v St Pauli while Schalke against Dortmund is the big clash between the two most popular teams from the Ruhr area.

Is it true that some Turkish clubs travel to a different continent to play a local derby?
Yes indeed – strange but true! Istanbul sides Besiktas and Galatasaray are based in the European side of the city while rivals Fenerbahce's home is across the Bosphorus strait, in the Asiatic part of the conurbation.

THE COLOURS

Before England played Germany in the semi-final of Euro 96 there was a big campaign to get them to play in red. Why was that?
A lot of people remember England winning the 1966 World Cup playing in red and wanted them to wear it against Germany. It also has to be said that the grey kit (officially called 'indigo blue') was not exactly popular either.

What other change colours have England worn?
Most England 'away' strips have been red although they have also sported yellow, sky blue and, of course, the 'indigo' jerseys. The sky blue strip they took to the 1970 World Cup finals in Mexico was so pale, they had to ditch it and recall their familiar red jerseys to provide a better contrast with quarter-final opponents West Germany.

Have Leeds always played in all white?
No. United's colours were blue and gold until Don Revie took over as manager in 1961. Revie declared that he wanted Leeds to be as great as Real Madrid and therefore changed their strip to all white – the same as the Spanish giants.

What about Liverpool's famous all-red strip?
Originally, the Anfield side played in a white shirt with a red V collar before switching to their familiar red shirt after a few years. White shorts and socks were worn until the mid-1960s when they adopted all-red after first using it for a European Cup tie against Anderlecht.

Have any other clubs changed their colours?

Although kit designs obviously change frequently
nowadays, few major clubs have actually altered their first-
choice colours in modern times. The last to do so in
Scotland were Dundee United who switched from black-and-
white to tangerine in the late 1960s. Apparently, United had
sported the tangerine kit while playing in an American
tournament and liked it so much they decided to adopt it as
their regular strip.

**How many different colours of strip have Manchester
United worn in recent years?**

I make it six. As well as their first-choice red, United have
played in white, black, blue, grey and green-and-yellow
halves over the past five or six seasons. The green-and-
yellow strip was introduced to commemorate the original
colours of Newton Heath, the club which was eventually to
become United.

What is the most common shirt colour in British football?

In England it's red, but blue is more common in Scotland.

**Is it true that Celtic's jerseys had no numbers until
recently?**

True – they wore their numbers on their shorts until the
League forced them to change in 1994. In fact, prior to 1960,
Celtic players weren't numbered at all.

When were numbers first introduced then?

Arsenal and Chelsea are both said to have experimented
with numbering in 1928 but it wasn't until 1939 that it
became compulsory in English football.

The famous Dutch star Johan Cruyff always wore No.14, didn't he?
Whenever he could. In Dutch football it wasn't a problem but when he played in Spanish soccer for Barcelona, the numbering was strictly 1–11 and so Cruyff wore No.9.

When did sponsored jerseys come in?
Following the lead of several European clubs, Liverpool became the first English League club to announce a shirt sponsorship deal (with *Hitachi*) in 1979. In Scotland, Hibs were the pioneers – they first sported the *Bukta* trade name during 1977–78.

Is it true that Hibs copied their white sleeves from Arsenal's jersey?
Yes it is. It was during the 1930s, when Arsenal were very much England's top dogs, that Hibs decided to adopt the Gunners-style jerseys.

Has any team ever played a match wearing their opponents' kit?
This has actually happened quite a few times over the years. As recently as March and April 1997, Birmingham City had to play two away First Division matches, at Crystal Palace and Oldham, in strips borrowed from their hosts. Ironically, Birmingham beat Palace wearing the 'unlucky' yellow jerseys which hadn't brought the Londoners a single victory in six outings!

Can you think of any other embarrassing moments with strips?
Fiorentina changed their away jerseys during 1992–93 after it was pointed out that the pattern on them resembled a Nazi-style swastika. Meanwhile in 1996, Ilkeston Ladies FC

ditched their white shorts for red because the old ones were see-through!

Do the Luxembourg team Red Boys Differdange actually play in red?
Yes!

DID YOU KNOW?

⚽ Queen's Park almost pulled out of a 1992 American tour match when an over-fussy referee insisted that their players break with the club's century-old tradition of wearing their shirts outside their shorts.

⚽ Tottenham made a real gaffe with their kit in the 1987 FA Cup final. Six of their team wore jerseys from which the sponsors' name was missing!

⚽ When Brighton adopted matching striped shirts and shorts in 1991, one critic likened them to 'a bunch of crazed Andy Pandys'!

⚽ During the early 1970s, Birmingham City players wore individualised shorts. Their initials – *T.F.*, *B.L.* etc. – were embroidered in blue at the bottom.

⚽ It takes about a metre of fabric to make a Rangers replica top. Enough are sold every year to stretch all the way from Glasgow to Edinburgh – and back.

PENALTIES

Has the penalty-kick always been part of the Laws of the Game?
No, it wasn't introduced until 1891, some 20 years after the FA Cup had begun. Wolves' John Heath became the first Football League player to convert a penalty when he scored against Accrington in September 1891.

What's the most penalties ever awarded in a English League match?
Referee Kelvin Morton awarded five penalties in the March 1989 Crystal Palace v Brighton game. Palace missed three of their four awards while Brighton converted their kick. The home side won 2–1.

What about in a match abroad?
Six penalties were awarded and converted during the Spanish *Primera Liga* clash between Oviedo and Valladolid of May 1996. Valladolid won 8–3 and their Croatian striker Peternec netted four of his five goals from the spot.

What's the record number of successful penalties taken by one player during a Football League season?
No-one has beaten the achievement of Francis Lee who put away 13 spot-kicks for Manchester City during 1971–72. He became known as 'Lee Won Pen' after the goal listing which would always be in the papers: Lee (1 pen)!

Who has been the penalty-king of Scottish football?
Arguably, that accolade should go to Rangers' 1950s star Johnny Hubbard. The South African winger was on target

with an amazing 54 of the 57 penalties that he took.

What about from the goalkeeping point of view. What's been the best performance on penalties?
Ipswich 'keeper Paul Cooper had a wonderful record during 1979–80. He managed to save eight of the ten kicks he faced – an unbelievably high percentage.

When did the penalty shoot-out become a part of cup football?
The shoot-out was introduced by UEFA in 1970 to decide deadlocked European ties. Slovakian side Spartak Trnava became the first team to progress in this way after they converted more spot-kicks than Fairs Cup opponents Marseille. Manchester United were the first shoot-out winners in British football – The Reds eliminated Hull City from the semi-finals of the sponsored Watney Cup tournament in August 1970.

What is Rangers' record in European penalty shoot-outs?
It's a brief but very interesting one. In 1972 the Gers became the first team to LOSE a penalty shoot-out and still progress in European competition. They thought they were out of the Cup-Winners' Cup when they went down on spot-kicks to Sporting Lisbon but they had in fact already won the tie on AWAY GOALS. The referee had been mistaken in ordering the shoot-out.

Which was the first team to win a major European club final after a shoot-out?
That was Valencia who defeated Arsenal 5–4 on penalties after the 1980 Cup-Winners' Cup final had ended 0–0.

Has any team missed all their kicks in a European final shoot-out?
Yes. In 1986, Barcelona missed four spot-kicks as they lost the penalty decider of their Champions' Cup final against Steaua Bucharest.

What is the record of British teams in final shoot-outs?
Although Arsenal lost in 1980, Liverpool and Tottenham both came through in their 1984 shoot-outs against Roma and Anderlecht respectively.

Apart from the 1994 World Cup, have any other major international competitions ever been settled on penalties?
The first was the 1976 European Championship final in which Czechoslovakia beat West Germany 5–3 on spot-kicks after a 2–2 draw. In 1995, Uruguay took the Copa America after a shoot-out while the Asian Cup, the Central American Gold Cup and the African Cup of Nations have all been decided in this way.

Is it true that France were once awarded a goal in a World Cup penalty shoot-out which shouldn't have been allowed?
Yes, that was in the 1986 quarter-final against Brazil. Bruno Bellone's shot rebounded from the post and therefore, according to the rules at the time, the ball was technically 'dead' before it hit Brazilian goalkeeper Carlos and bounced back into goal. The rules have since been amended to allow the ball to finish its flight.

What's the highest score ever recorded in a penalty shoot-out?
In November 1988, Argentinos Juniors beat Racing Club Avellaneda 20–19 in a marathon shoot-out to decide a drawn

Argentinian League match. In British football, 28 kicks were taken before Aldershot eventually defeated Fulham 11–10 in a 1987 Freight Rover Trophy tie.

Why do the Germans call a penalty-kick *'ein Elfmeter'*?
Elf meter is eleven metres – the metric equivalent of the 12-yard distance from which penalties are taken.

MANAGERS

Who's been the most successful manager in English football?
That has to be Bob Paisley who guided Liverpool to an unbelievable haul of honours during his nine-year reign at Anfield. The Reds won six League Championships, three European Cups, three League Cups, one UEFA Cup and one European Super Cup.

Kenny Dalglish managed both Liverpool and Blackburn Rovers to the League Championship. Has anyone else steered two clubs to the title?
Only two others have achieved that feat – Herbert Chapman (with Huddersfield and Arsenal during the inter-war period) and Brian Clough (with Derby in 1972 and Nottingham Forest in '78).

Has any manager won all four English divisional championships?
No, but Sir Alf Ramsey comes closest. Between 1957 and 1962, he guided Ipswich Town to the Third, Second and First Division titles.

Who was the first-ever player-manager?
That was Andy Cunningham of Newcastle United in 1930. When Graeme Souness joined the Rangers board in November 1988, he became British football's first player-manager-director.

What's the shortest-ever reign by a manager at an English League club?
Bill Lambton only lasted three days at Scunthorpe in April 1959. Maybe it was something he said!

Which English League club has had the most managers?
Wigan certainly take that dubious honour in the post-war era having had no less than 31 bosses since 1946.

And which club has had the fewest?
West Ham. When Harry Redknapp succeeded Billy Bonds in 1994 he became only the Hammers' eighth boss in 101 years.

Which current English League manager has been at his club the longest?
At the end of 1996–97, it was Dario Gradi who celebrated 14 years at Crewe by leading the club to promotion from Division Two. Among the Premiership teams, Alex Ferguson is the longest-serving boss, having arrived at Old Trafford in November 1986.

Who's the longest-serving coach in European football?
I would doubt if many can beat Guy Roux who first took charge of AJ Auxerre in 1961!

Which major British manager has been in charge of the most clubs?
It's probably Tommy Docherty who, in addition to eight Football League teams, also bossed Scotland, Porto, Altrincham and two Australian sides – no wonder he said he'd had more clubs than Jack Nicklaus! Of the current bosses, the 'Bald Eagle' Jim Smith has been in charge of eight clubs – Birmingham, Blackburn, Colchester, Newcastle, Oxford, Portsmouth, QPR and, most recently, Derby.

Who's been the most successful British manager abroad?
Since 1990, Bobby Robson has won the Dutch and
Portuguese championships and the European Cup-Winners'
Cup. Arguably however, Roy Hodgson comes close to
equalling Robson's accomplishments. Hodgson captured
four Swedish titles with Halmstads and Malmo, took the
Swiss national team to the 1994 World Cup and 1996
European Championships and had a UEFA Cup near-miss
with Inter Milan in 1997.

**Ruud Gullit masterminded Chelsea's success in the 1997
FA Cup. Was he the first foreign manager to lead a team
out in a Wembley cup final?**
No, that first was achieved by the Uruguayan Danny Bergara
who guided Stockport County to the 1992 Autoglass Trophy
final.

**The McLean brothers, Jim and Tommy, were long-term
managerial rivals in Scottish football. Are there any
brothers currently managing in England?**
Yes, Brian and Alan Little who in 1996–97 were the bosses of
Aston Villa and York respectively.

**Would it be fair to say that great players don't always
make good managers?**
While people like Pelé and Bobby Charlton obviously didn't
hit it off in management, there are plenty of other examples
of great players who've gone on to enjoy outstanding
success in a managerial capacity. Names like Johan Cruyff,
Franz Beckenbauer and, of course, Kenny Dalglish spring to
mind.

Many of the old-school managers like Bill Shankly and Jock Stein were renowned for their psychology. What kind of tricks did they play?
I like the one attributed to Jock Stein before Celtic's home European Cup tie with Red Star Belgrade in 1968. Big Jock knew that winger Jimmy Johnstone was terrified of flying and made a deal with the wee man that he would leave him out of the return match if Celtic built up a handsome lead at home. Johnstone apparently played an absolute blinder and inspired his team to a 5–1 victory!

Has any manager ever been sacked while being 'Manager of the Month'?
Mike Walker achieved that unique double at Colchester in October 1987.

ALLY'S TOP TEN

Ten men who have managed Scotland...

Andy Beattie (Feb–Jun 1954 and Mar 1959–Oct 1960)
Ian McColl (Nov 1960–May 1965)
Jock Stein (Jun–Dec 1965 and Oct 1978–Sep 1985)
Bobby Brown (Feb 1967–Jun 1971)
Tommy Docherty (Oct 1971–Dec 1972)
Willie Ormond (Jan 1973–Apr 1977)
Ally MacLeod (May 1977–Oct 1978)
Alex Ferguson (Sep 1985–Jun 1986)
Andy Roxburgh (Jul 1986–Sep 1993)
Craig Brown (Sep 1993–)

TV HEAVEN

When was the first televised football match?
The BBC shot some TV footage of Arsenal's game with
Everton in August 1936 but it's thought that the Germany v
Italy international, some three months later, was the first
match to be screened live.

What about the FA Cup final?
Part of the 1937 Preston v Sunderland final went out live but
the following year's Preston-Huddersfield match was the
first final to be transmitted in its entirety. The first live
Scottish Cup final was Clyde v Celtic in 1955. Incidentally,
Clyde's scorer in that game, Archie Robertson, later became
a chemistry teacher and coach of my school team!

When did *Match of the Day* begin?
It was first broadcast in August 1964 on BBC 2. It featured
Liverpool v West Ham from Anfield and 'Pool's Roger Hunt
scored the first-ever goal seen on the programme.
Apparently, the audience for the first show was only around
22,000.

Has *Match of the Day* run continuously since then?
More or less. There was a spell between 1988 and 1992 when
ITV had exclusive rights to League matches and so *Match of
the Day* was only screened on days when there was FA Cup
football on.

When did League matches first appear live?
Blackpool v Bolton in September 1960 was the first League
game to be beamed live. However regular live coverage of

English League matches didn't really begin until October
1983 when ITV screened Tottenham v Nottingham Forest.

What about Scottish League games?
The first live Premier League fixture was Hearts v Aberdeen
in April 1986. In August that year, Rangers won the first-ever
live Old Firm League clash when my good pal Ian Durrant
slotted home the game's only goal.

When did satellite TV appear on the scene?
The first major league fixture to be screened live in Britain
via satellite was the Old Firm match of April 1990 which was
featured on BSB. (We won 3–0!)

What financial impact did the advent of satellite have on the game?
A huge one. The money that Sky and the BBC put up to cover
the Premier League in 1992 was about seven times as much
as ITV's previous deal with the old Football League. The
latest joint agreement, made in June 1996, is worth an
incredible £743 million over four seasons – a record TV
contract for British sport.

How many cameras do Sky use when they cover a Premiership match live?
Usually about 15. Altogether around 70 people are involved
in the broadcast operation which is controlled from a huge
truck outside the ground.

When was the World Cup first covered by television?
The 1954 finals in Switzerland were the first to be televised.
Unfortunately, Scotland's live TV debut, in the group match
against Uruguay, turned out to be a real X-rated show as the
Dark Blues crashed 7–0!

When were the finals first broadcast in colour?
That was in 1970 when Mexico hosted the tournament for the first time. As in 1986, the matches were timed to fit in with European TV schedules so many of the games kicked off at noon when it was a wee bit on the hot side!

How many viewers watched the 1994 World Cup finals?
USA 94 had a total TV audience of 31.7 billion. It's estimated that a record-breaking 37 billion will watch the 1998 finals in France.

That famous line 'They think it's all over' comes from a piece of TV football commentary. Who said it and when?
It was Kenneth Wolstenholme near the end of the BBC's coverage of the 1966 World Cup final. With England 3–2 ahead and Geoff Hurst bearing down on the West German goal, several fans had ran onto the park in the belief that time was up. Wolstenholme remarked: 'Some people are on the pitch, they think it's all over…' and then, as Hurst scored to seal England's victory, he quipped: '… it is now!'

Which commentators have played football themselves?
Sky Sports' Martin Tyler was a striker with Corinthian Casuals but the most unusual first-hand experience probably belongs to my former *A Question of Sport* colleague David Coleman who once made a guest appearance for Stockport County reserves!

HAT-TRICKS

What's the origin of the term 'hat-trick'?
Football really borrowed the expression from cricket which had a tradition that a bowler who took three wickets in three deliveries was rewarded with a new hat. Originally a footballer needed to score three consecutive goals before being credited with a 'hat-trick'.

Who scored the world's first-ever competitive hat-trick?
The earliest recorded examples are the trebles scored by Wanderers players Kingsford and Wollaston and Oxford University's Parry in a first round match of the 1874–75 FA Cup tournament. The first Football League hat-trick was notched by Walter Tait of Burnley against Bolton in September 1888.

What about in Scotland?
Rangers' John McPherson claimed the original Scottish League hat-trick when he bagged four goals in a 6–2 Gers' win at Cambuslang in August 1890.

Who holds the record for the most hat-tricks in a season?
George Camsell of Middlesbrough hit no less than nine during 1926–27. Rangers' Jim Forrest banged in eight trebles in 1964–65, five in the League and three in the League Cup.

Which player has hit the most hat-tricks in a single Premiership season?
Alan Shearer scored five for Blackburn during 1995–96. Jimmy Greaves holds the post-war record for the top flight with six hat-tricks for Chelsea in 1960–61.

When did three players last score a hat-trick for one team during the same League match?
That was in November 1987 when Tony Adcock, Paul Stewart and David White all bagged three goals in Manchester City's 10–1 trouncing of Huddersfield Town.

Which British player holds the record for the most career hat-tricks?
The famous Bill 'Dixie' Dean is credited with 37 hat-tricks, more than any other player.

Is Geoff Hurst the only man to have hit a hat-trick for England in the World Cup finals?
No, Gary Lineker notched all three goals in the 1986 first round victory against Poland in Mexico.

Which player has scored the most hat-tricks for England?
That's Jimmy Greaves with six. Gary Lineker comes next on five.

Which player holds the record for the quickest hat-trick in British football?
Jock Dodds of Blackpool who, in February 1943, put three goals past Tranmere Rovers in only two-and-a-half minutes. However, Ian St John is believed to have matched that timing with his treble for Motherwell against Hibs at Easter Road in August 1959.

What's the fastest hat-trick of all time?
The record stands at 1 minute and 50 seconds by Maglioni of Independiente against fellow Argentinians Gimnasia in March 1973.

Who was the last player to score a hat-trick in a European competition final?
That was Jupp Heynckes for Borussia Monchengladbach in the second leg of the 1975 UEFA Cup final. Heynckes' threesome against FC Twente Enschede took his goals total for the tournament to eleven.

Has any player ever scored a hat-trick in a Champions' Cup final yet still finished on the losing side?
Incredibly, Ferenc Puskas did that when Real Madrid lost 5–3 to Benfica in Amsterdam in 1962. The last player to score three goals in a Champions' Cup final was AC Milan's Pierino Prati against Ajax in 1969.

Is it correct that Scottish international John Wark once scored a hat-trick of penalties for Ipswich Town, and is that unique?
John Wark did indeed convert three spot-kicks during a 1980 UEFA Cup game against Aris Salonika. The feat has however been achieved by several players, including Jan Molby for Liverpool against Coventry in 1986. Rangers' Willie Johnston almost did it in November 1971 when his hat-trick against St Johnstone came from two cleanly-converted penalties and one rebound from the spot.

Gordon Durie hit a hat-trick for Rangers in the 1996 Scottish Cup final against Hearts. Have there been any other final hat-tricks?
Only two – both by Celtic strikers. Jimmy Quinn scored all three goals against Rangers in 1904 while Dixie Deans notched his treble in the 6–1 win over Hibs of 1972. Celtic's Dixie was no relation to the famous Everton star but was simply nicknamed after him.

Has any player ever scored a hat-trick of headers?
Again that's been done a few times. Four of Malcolm
Macdonald's five goals for England against Cyprus in 1975
came from his head while Czechoslovakia's Tomas Skuhravy
nodded a World Cup finals hat-trick against Costa Rica in
1990.

DID YOU KNOW?

⚽ Alan Shearer scored a hat-trick on his full League debut
for Southampton against Arsenal in April 1988.

⚽ When Allan Johnston hit all three goals in Hearts'
January 1996 win over Rangers at Ibrox, he became the
first visiting player to complete a hat-trick since St
Mirren's Ally McLeod scored four goals in a League Cup
tie of August 1972.

⚽ Manchester United's David Herd scored a hat-trick past
three different goalkeepers as United defeated
Sunderland 5–0 in November 1966.

⚽ In February 1997, midfielder Ray McKinnon fired an
unusual hat-trick of free-kicks to help Dundee United to a
3–2 Premier League victory at Kilmarnock.

TACTICS

What formations did teams use in the early days of football?
The line-up usually consisted of a goalkeeper, a 'three-quarter-back', a half-back and EIGHT forwards.

And what were the playing tactics?
There were little team tactics as such. The usual pattern was that a player simply dribbled with the ball until he lost it and then a team-mate would hopefully be on hand to back him up.

So there was no passing?
Initially no. It was reputedly the Scots who first realised that it might be a good idea to pass the ball before you were tackled.

So when the passing game eventually took off, were the teams that played with only one or two defenders not simply over-run?
Yes they were and several sides therefore experimented with new defensive systems. Cambridge University in 1877 were among the first to use two full-backs and three half-backs.

When did teams first use central defenders as we know them?
In 1925, after a change in the offside law gave an extra benefit to the attacking side, many teams withdrew their middle half-back to play as a central defender between the two full-backs. At the same time, the midfield area was bolstered by the two inside-forwards who dropped deeper.

Was that a 3–4–3 formation then?
More or less. The next significant change was developed by the Hungarians who added another central defender, pulled back their centre-forward and pushed up the inside-forwards into a twin-striking role supported by the wingers. This was known as 4–2–4 and it was also the system used by Brazil when they won the World Cup in 1958.

That sounds like an adventurous formation. Why did it not last?
As the stakes became higher during the 1960s, managers and coaches grew more cautious and 4–2–4 evolved into 4–3–3 and then 4–4–2. Obviously forward power had to be sacrificed to strengthen the defence and many teams dispensed with the position of winger.

What tactics did England's 1966 World Cup winning side use?
With no real top-class wingers at his disposal, Alf Ramsey developed a 4–3–3 system which simply didn't require them. When England defended the trophy four years later in Mexico, Sir Alf employed a 4–4–2 formation with the idea that his overlapping full-backs would compensate for the absence of wide players. Ironically, the goal that ended England's reign was set up by some individual magic from West German winger Jurgen Grabowski.

Italian teams enjoyed a lot of success with the *catenaccio* defensive system. How did that come about?
Catenaccio, which incidentally means 'door-chain', evolved from a system developed in Switzerland and known as 'The Bolt'. The key feature of *catenaccio* is the sweeper, a defender who plays behind a line of three or four man-marking defenders with the sole task of clearing up any danger if the line is breached.

Franz Beckenbauer was a sweeper but he used to venture upfield regularly. Why was that?

The Germans and the Dutch really pioneered the idea of the attacking sweeper or 'libero'. Beckenbauer was such a talented player and a marvellous reader of the game that he was a potent attacking weapon for both his club Bayern Munich and West Germany.

What other developments came about in the 1960s?

Set-piece moves which entered the game included two variations on corner-kicks – the short corner and the near-post corner. The short corner was designed to improve the angle of the cross while the near-post corner was exploited by strong aerial players such as Jack Charlton to set up goal chances for team-mates. I can actually remember working on short corners with my school team which was quite innovative for that age group.

What was 'Total Football'?

That was the tag given to the fluid and exciting style used especially by Ajax Amsterdam and Holland during the early 1970s. Because they had multi-talented squads, everyone was considered to be a potential attacker or indeed defender and the players regularly interchanged positions at will.

What's the most common formation nowadays?

Many teams use a 5–3–2 or 5–3–1–1 system which is designed to allow the two wing-backs to push up into midfield to make more of a 3–5–2 set up. Some sides however, prefer to stick with a flat back-four defence and line up either 4–4–2 or 4–5–1.

WORLD SOCCER

Brazil have won four World Cup tournaments. Have they been as successful in their own South American Championship?
Relatively speaking, nowhere near as successful. Brazil have won only five of the 39 Copa America competitions held between 1910 and 1997. Argentina lead the way with 15 victories closely followed by Uruguay's 14.

What is South America's premier club event?
That's the Copa Libertadores de América. It began in 1960 and was very much inspired by the European Champions' Cup tournament.

Which team has won the Copa Libertadores most often?
Independiente of Argentina, who enjoyed seven victories between 1964 and 1984. Uruguay's Penarol come next with five triumphs.

Because of its altitude, the Bolivian capital La Paz was, for a while, banned from staging World Cup matches. Is it the highest football venue in the world?
No, Peruvian club side Union Minas can make the lofty claim of the world's highest senior football ground – 4,350 metres (nearly 14,300 feet) above sea-level!

Have South American teams won the World Club Cup more often than their European counterparts?
Yes. Between 1960 and 1996 the cup went to South America 20 times with European sides winning on 15 occasions.

Is it true that the World Club Cup final has a history of violence?

Yes, especially in the late 1960s. In 1967, six players were ordered off during the Racing Club v Celtic decider in Montevideo. Two years later, things deteriorated to such an extent that three players from Argentinian side Estudiantes were IMPRISONED after a brutal match against AC Milan.

Have any British players ever starred in South American soccer?

Very few. The most famous was probably England centre-half Neil Franklin who quit Stoke City in May 1950 to play in Colombia's big-money 'pirate' league.

Major League Soccer began in the United States in 1996. Is this the first time that the Americans have had a professional football set-up?

No – but for some reason they have never managed to establish a league of any durability. Since 1920, there have been the ASL, EPL, GASL, ISL, NPSL, NASL, CSL, USL, MISL and APSL! The most successful was the NASL (North American Soccer League) in which several world superstars such as Pelé and Johan Cruyff played before large audiences in the major US cities. The NASL eventually collapsed in 1985.

Which team won the first MLS championship?

Washington DC United defeated Los Angeles Galaxy 3–2 in the first-ever final, held in Foxboro in October 1996. Washington were captained by the former Sheffield Wednesday and Derby player John Harkes.

Cameroon took the World Cup by storm in 1990. Were they the first African side to compete in the finals?

No, that was Egypt as far back as 1934. Interestingly enough, one of their team, Mohammed Latif, signed for Rangers later in the year.

Who's the most famous African-born player of all-time?
Arguably that would be Eusebio, the explosive forward who was born in the former Portuguese colony of Mozambique. Eusebio averaged more than a goal a game for Lisbon giants Benfica and also hit 41 goals in 64 appearances for Portugal.

George Weah was voted European Footballer of the Year in 1995 – but was he not born in Africa?
He's from Liberia but the voting regulations have been changed to include any player with a European club. Weah is just one of many Africans who are currently starring in European soccer.

When did Japan's J-League begin?
It started in 1993 and the inaugural championship was won by Verdy Kawasaki.

Gary Lineker played for the Japanese team Nagoya Grampus Eight. Why are they so-called?
The Grampus was a killer whale which, according to legend, saved the city of Nagoya from fire by sprouting water from the sea.

Have Australia ever appeared in the World Cup finals?
Yes, in 1974. They lost to both East and West Germany but managed a respectable 0–0 draw with Chile.

Do the New Zealand football team play in the same all-black strip as their rugby counterparts?
No, they wear all-white and are known, funnily enough, as the All Whites!

How many countries are members of FIFA?
FIFA had 198 member countries in June 1997. 172 of them registered to compete in the qualifying competition for the 1998 World Cup tournament.

Which other countries have teams called 'Rangers'?
Some other 'Rangers' who have been champions of their country include Enugu Rangers (Nigeria), Manning Rangers (South Africa), Nchanga Rangers (Zambia) and Hong Kong Rangers. In Chile there's a club called Rangers Talca.

ALLY'S TOP TEN

Ten interesting team names from around the world…

The Strongest (Bolivia)
Mighty Blackpool (Sierra Leone)
Dangerous Darkies (South Africa)
Invincible Eleven (Liberia)
Always Ready (Bolivia)
Fire Brigade (Mauritius)
Shooting Stars (Nigeria)
Eleven Men in Flight (Swaziland)
Mysterious Dwarves (Ghana)
FC Horsed (Somalia)

REFEREES

Who was the English referee who controlled the 1974 World Cup final?
That was Jack Taylor, a master butcher from Wolverhampton. Taylor bravely awarded Holland a penalty in the first minute of the match.

Was he the first Briton to referee a World Cup final?
No, Bill Ling handled the 1954 final while George Reader was in charge of the deciding match of the 1950 World Cup tournament, between Brazil and Uruguay. Ironically, at the time Mr Reader was considered 'too old' to referee English League games.

Who is the most famous British referee of all time?
That's almost certainly Sir Stanley Rous who went on to serve as President of FIFA between 1961 and 1974. A well-respected ref, he handled the 1934 FA Cup final and no less than 36 international matches. Probably Scotland's best-known official is Tom 'Tiny' Wharton, an imposing figure who took charge of 23 Old Firm matches during his career.

Why are linesman now called 'assistant referees'?
The change was made by FIFA in 1996 to more accurately reflect the role of the linesman and also to be more politically correct.

The Premier League appointed their first female official in 1997. Who is she?
She's Wendy Toms from Poole and she has already refereed Vauxhall Conference matches and ran the line in the Nationwide League.

Is it true that Paul Gascoigne was once booked for showing the referee his own yellow card?

That was exactly what happened during Rangers' December 1995 Premier League match against Hibs. After referee Dougie Smith had dropped his yellow card, Gazza picked it up and jokingly waved it at the official. Unfortunately, the ref didn't see the funny side and promptly returned the compliment.

What's the strangest booking of all time?

There are a few contenders but here are a couple. Shrewsbury's Vic Kasule was once yellow carded for whistling a George Benson song when he should've been taking a corner while, in 1996, Italian non-league player Marco Bochetti was cautioned before he had even come onto the pitch – for relieving himself behind the dugout!

Which player holds the record for the quickest booking ever?

Vinnie Jones was yellow-carded after only THREE SECONDS while playing for Chelsea against Sheffield United in an FA Cup tie of February 1992. A year or so earlier, Vinnie had eased himself into the game a bit more with a five-second caution in Sheffield United's League match at Manchester City.

Has a referee ever booked all 22 players during a match?

Believe it or not, yes! In a 1969 game between Tongham Youth Club and Hawley, the ref cautioned every single player – then booked the linesman for dissent!

What's the worst show of dissent ever made to a referee by a player?

There's a fairly extreme example from a 1994 amateur game

in Edinburgh in which a player, having being sent off, dived into his car and drove speedily across the pitch towards the poor ref. Sounds as if he wasn't quite in full agreement with the decision!

Who is Scotland's best referee?

Hugh Dallas came top of the UEFA rankings in 1997 but a 1989 *Rangers News* questionnaire on the subject produced an interesting response. 6.9% of readers voted for Aberdeen captain Willie Miller!

Have the authorities ever experimented with the idea of using more than one referee to control the match?

It was actually suggested at the AGM of the Football League in 1935 and, although the concept was tried in a couple of representative matches that year, it never really mustered enough support.

How much are referees paid for handling a Premiership match?

The fee in 1997–98 was £375 for a referee and £165 for an assistant. That compares quite favourably with the 52.5 pence that refs received in 1888.

What's the most common occupation among officials on the National List of Referees?

Schoolteacher.

Who was the most appropriately-named referee of all time?

I think that has to be the Scottish World Cup ref of the 1950s – Charlie Faultless. Incidentally, there was once an Austrian referee called Herr Frankenstein. Eric Hall would no doubt say he was a monster official!

How many miles does a referee cover during a match?
According to the official FIFA guidelines on fitness, a ref needs to be able to run about eight miles during the course of a game.

Has a referee ever scored a goal?
Yes. During a 1968 match between Barrow and Plymouth, unfortunate man-in-black Ivan Robinson inadvertently deflected a cross past Plymouth goalkeeper Pat Dunne for the only goal of the game!

— DEBUTS

What's the best debut performance of all-time in English football?
In terms of goalscoring, it must be Len Shackleton's six goals on his Newcastle debut against Newport in 1946. In Scotland, Jim Dyet notched eight for King's Park against Forfar in 1930.

What's the most goals scored by any player in his first Football League match?
The record is five by Chelsea's George Hilsdon in a 9–2 win over Glossop in a Second Division match of September 1906.

Is it true that Jimmy Greaves scored in his debut match for each of his clubs?
Yes, Greavsie netted on his debut for Chelsea, AC Milan, Tottenham and West Ham. He even scored on his first international appearance for England against Peru in 1959.

What is the most impressive debut ever made by a Rangers player?
Probably that by Colin Stein who hit three goals in four minutes at Arbroath in November 1968. Thirteen years earlier winger Alex Scott notched a hat-trick on his Gers debut against his home town team Falkirk.

Has any player ever been sent off on his Scottish League debut?
Rangers player-manager Graeme Souness hit the headlines when he was ordered off after just 37 minutes of his Premier League debut, against Hibs at Easter Road in August 1986.

What's the most unfortunate debut ever made?
There have been a few rather sad first outings.
Northampton Town's Bert Llewellyn spent only 11 minutes
on the pitch before injury ended his spell with the club
while Halifax goalkeeper Stanley Milton let in thirteen goals
on his debut in 1934.

What's been the most sensational debut by a goalkeeper?
Probably that of Tony Coton who saved a penalty after only
85 seconds of his first League match for Birmingham City
against Sunderland in December 1980. A few months earlier,
Aberdeen's Belgian goalkeeper Marc de Clerck actually
SCORED with a long kick-out on his club debut at Berwick
Rangers.

**Has any League club fielded an entire team of debutants
in a match?**
No, that's of course excluding clubs who were playing in
their first League match. However, Rochdale had ten
debutants in their side for a Third Division North game
against Carlisle in 1932.

**What's the most impressive debut performance by an
England player?**
I can't see anyone ever topping that of Aston Villa's Howard
Vaughton who banged in five goals during the 13–0 demoli-
tion of Ireland in 1882. The best post-war debut haul was the
four scored by Stan Mortensen against Portugal in 1947.

Did Alan Shearer score on his international debut?
Alan's first full international appearance was against France
in February 1992 and he notched the opening goal in
England's 2–0 win. He had previously found the net on his
debut for the England Youth, Under-21 and B teams.

Is it true that a player once scored for Scotland without having kicked a ball in international football?
Joe Craig accomplished that unique feat against Sweden in April 1977. Coming on as a substitute for Kenny Burns, the Celtic striker headed a goal with his first touch.

What's the quickest debut goal ever scored by an England player?
The record is shared by Jack Cock (in 1919) and Bill Nicholson (in 1951) who both took no longer than 30 seconds to open their international account.

Has any player ever made his England debut in a World Cup finals match?
The last to do so was Leeds' Allan Clarke who actually scored the only goal of the 1970 first round clash against Czechoslovakia in Mexico.

Has any player ever made his international debut before playing a League match for his club?
Several have, usually Northern Ireland or Republic of Ireland players. A good recent example is Keith Gillespie who started for Northern Ireland against Portugal in September 1994, a month before making his Premiership debut for Manchester United at Sheffield Wednesday.

Has any player ever made his senior debut in a major cup final?
On example is Jim Denny who was a shock debutant for Rangers in the 1971 Scottish Cup final replay against Celtic. Denny was called up to replace broken-jaw victim Alex Miller.

What's the worst start ever made by a manager in international football?
In British terms, it must be that of Willie Ormond whose debut as Scotland boss in February 1973 could hardly have been more drastic. The Scots crashed 5–0 to England at Hampden.

ALLY'S TOP TEN

Ten players who scored on their League debut for Rangers...

Dave Smith (1966)
Orjan Persson (1967)
Iain MacDonald (1970)
Bobby Russell (1977)
Robert Prytz (1982)
Gary Stevens (1988)
Neale Cooper (1988)
Mel Sterland (1989)
Mark Hateley (1990)
Dale Gordon (1991)

A QUESTION OF SPORTS

Who was the most famous footballing cricketer?
Arguably it was Denis Compton, the Middlesex and England
batsman who was also the left-winger in Arsenal's FA Cup
winning side of 1950. Denis made one footballing
appearance for England in a wartime international.

Wasn't there another Compton brother?
Yes, Leslie Compton was also a dual performer with
Middlesex and Arsenal. Centre-half Les won his first football
cap at the age of 38, making him the oldest England debutant
of all time.

Does Andy Goram still play cricket?
Because of his football contract, he can't at the moment.
Andy has played cricket for Scotland and actually hit four
runs in a 1989 international against Australia. Former
Rangers player and manager Scot Symon was also a double
internationalist at football and cricket.

**Who was the last player to appear in a Test match at Lord's
and an FA Cup final at Wembley?**
That was Mick Lambert who was Ipswich Town's substitute
in the 1978 FA Cup final. Ten years earlier, while a youngster
on the MCC groundstaff, Mick had fielded as England's 12th
man during a match against Australia. That's a fairly unique
substitution double.

Has anyone ever played first-class cricket and League football on the same day?
Amazingly yes! On 15 September 1975, Test cricketer Chris Balderstone batted for Leicestershire against Derbyshire in the morning and appeared for Doncaster Rovers against Brentford in the afternoon!

Have there ever been any joint football and rugby internationalists?
Several, including England goalkeepers Charles Wilson and John Sutcliffe. Others capped at both codes were the Scotsman Henry Renny-Tailyour and the Irish brothers Kevin and Michael O'Flanagan.

Why are there football stadia with names like Rugby Park and The Racecourse Ground?
Rugby Park is so-called because Kilmarnock played rugby for a while before eventually switching to soccer while Wrexham's Racecourse Ground was developed on the site of a racecourse. Derby County's former home, The Baseball Ground, was first laid out by a foundry owner who, on his return from a spell in the USA, tried to introduce the American sport to his workers.

Which sports other than football has Wembley staged?
Wembley has also hosted rugby, athletics, American football, hockey, speedway, greyhound racing and show jumping. The 1969 League Cup final was played on a surface which had been badly churned up by the Royal International Horse Show.

Which top European footballers have been stars in other sports?
The legendary Dynamo Moscow and Soviet Union

goalkeeper Lev Yashin was nearly lost to football when, during the early part of his career, he considered concentrating on ice hockey. The 1950s Yugoslavian star Branko Zebec was a talented all-round sprinter and long-jumper.

Several European clubs run teams in other sports. Have any British clubs ever done that?
Both Rangers and Manchester United have in the past fielded basketball sides.

Who's the former England striker who became a successful racehorse trainer?
That's Mick Channon. Other well-known soccer personalities with an involvement in the Sport of Kings include Alan Ball, Kevin Keegan and Francis Lee.

Has any Rangers player enjoyed major success at another sport?
One-time Ibrox reserve Bob Sutherland went on to become World Indoor Bowls champion.

How many top sports stars are football fans?
There are quite a few who follow their favourite teams. They include Steve Cram (Sunderland), Liz McColgan (Dundee United), Alec Stewart (Chelsea), Graham Gooch (West Ham), Brian Lara (Aston Villa), Sharron Davies (Plymouth Argyle), John Higgins (Celtic), Jimmy White (Chelsea), Andy Gregory (Manchester United) and Steve Collins (Celtic). I also mustn't forget my *A Question of Sport* rival John Parrott who's an avid Evertonian.

Who was Britain's greatest sporting all-rounder of all-time?

That has to be Charles (CB) Fry, the Southampton full-back who, besides being a double internationalist at football and cricket, also equalled the world long-jump record in 1893. For good measure, he played rugby for the Barbarians and was also said to have been a fine boxer, plus a passable golfer, swimmer, rower, tennis player and javelin thrower. All this seems to have impressed the Albanians so much that they are reputed to have asked CB to be their King!

GOALS AND GOALSCORERS

Who is the leading goalscorer in football history?
Brazilian Artur Friedenreich netted an incredible 1,329 goals
in a 26-year career between 1909 and 1935. He played for
Germania, Ipiranga, Americano, Paulistano, Sao Paulo,
Flamengo and the Brazilian national team.

What about Pelé, he can't have been far behind?
Pele is estimated to have scored 1,282 goals between 1956
and 1977. Some statisticians actually make him the top all-
time scorer but that would include numerous goals in
friendlies for his club Santos. He certainly holds the record
for most goals in a single season – 126 in 1959.

**Who is the all-time leading scorer in the English and
Scottish leagues?**
Arthur Rowley hit 434 goals for West Bromwich, Fulham,
Leicester and Shrewsbury between 1946 and 1965 while
Jimmy McGrory registered 410 goals in 408 appearances
with Celtic and Clydebank from 1922 to 1937. With 550 first-
class goals in all, McGrory is British football's record scorer
of all time.

**Has any player ever averaged more than a goal-a-game in
international football?**
Several players have managed this, especially during the
last century when there was some pretty high scoring. The
best ratio by a seasoned international in recent times is

undoubtedly that of Gerd Muller who netted 68 goals in 62 appearances for West Germany.

How many goals did Muller score in the World Cup finals?

'Der Bomber' hit 14 in all, including the winner in the 1974 final against Holland – his last match before his retirement from international football. That goal took him past Just Fontaine's record of 13 which was set in 1958.

Who's the leading goalscorer in the European Cup competition?

Real Madrid's Argentinian-born striker Alfredo di Stefano amassed a tournament record 49 goals between 1955 and 1964. Meanwhile, his team-mate Francisco 'Paco' Gento managed a goal in every one of Madrid's first eleven European Cup campaigns.

What's the most goals scored by one player in a first-class match?

Stephan Stanis of Lens is credited with 16 goals in a French Cup tie against Aubry-Asturies in December 1942. The British record is held by Arbroath centre-forward John Petrie who hit 13 in the famous 36–0 Scottish Cup win over Bon Accord in 1885. The last British player to reach double figures in a senior match was Gerry Baker who banged in ten for St Mirren during a January 1960 Scottish Cup tie against Glasgow University.

What's the best consecutive run of scoring by any player in British football?

That was achieved by the Danish forward Finn Dossing who netted in 15 games on the trot for Dundee United during 1964–65.

Roberto di Matteo rocketed Chelsea ahead after only 42 seconds of the 1997 FA Cup final. Was that Wembley's fastest goal of all time?
It certainly beat the previous record for a Wembley FA Cup final held by Jackie Milburn's 45-second goal for Newcastle United in 1955. However the fastest-ever goal in a first-class match at the Stadium remains the one scored by Bryan Robson after 38 seconds of England's December 1989 friendly against Yugoslavia.

What's the quickest goal ever scored?
Damian Mori of Adelaide City claimed that after he lobbed Sydney United goalkeeper John Perosh after only 3.69 seconds of an Australian National League match in December 1995. English football's fastest-ever goal is credited to Jim Fryatt who netted after four seconds while playing for Bradford Park Avenue against Tranmere in April 1964.

When did the Adidas Golden Boot award begin?
The Golden Boot (or Golden Shoe) competition was launched in 1967 as an annual prize to the top goalscorer in European football. The first winner was Eusebio who hit 43 Portuguese League goals for Benfica during 1967–68.

Which British players have won the Golden Boot?
Ian Rush was the first British recipient in 1983–84 and a certain A McCoist became the first player to win the award in consecutive seasons, in 1991–92 and 1992–93.

Does the competition still run along the same lines?
There were some major changes introduced in 1996. Now every goal scored in Europe's top leagues (i.e. countries nos. 1–8 in the UEFA ranking) is worth twice as much as

those in the leagues of the smaller countries. In addition, goals scored in countries ranked 9–21 are multiplied by a factor of 1.5. It sounds complicated but the idea is to reflect the differing standards among the various European leagues.

DID YOU KNOW?

⚽ Peter Aldis of Aston Villa is believed to have scored the longest headed goal ever in British football. On 1 September 1952, Aldis nodded the ball into the Sunderland net from all of 35 yards.

⚽ No less than NINE different Liverpool players were on the scoresheet during The Reds' 1974 European Cup-Winners' Cup first round, first leg match with Stromsgodset of Norway.

⚽ Women's football has also produced some impressive scoring feats. Linda Curl of Norwich Ladies chalked up 23 goals in a 40–0 win over Milton Keynes reserves in 1983.

⚽ In November 1922, Billy Minter of St Albans City scored seven goals in an FA Cup match yet still finished on the losing side! Dulwich Hamlet won the qualifying tie 8–7.

LAWS OF THE GAME

How many Laws of the Game are there?
Seventeen.

Who decides if any of the Laws are to be amended?
A body known as the International Board which was
founded in 1886. It's run jointly by FIFA and the four British
associations.

**Which Law has been the most controversial over the
years?**
Most people would say the offside law.

What is the idea behind the offside law?
It's really designed to prevent teams simply launching the
ball into a packed goalmouth.

What changes have been made to the law?
Prior to 1925 an attacking player was offside unless THREE
opponents were between him and the opposition goal at the
moment when the ball was played forward. In a significant
move, the ruling was changed that year to require only TWO
opponents to play the attacker onside.

What about the more recent changes?
The latest modifications have really been devised to sway
the balance in favour of the offensive side. The 1990 ruling
stated that a forward would no longer be judged offside if he
was LEVEL with the second-last opponent when the ball was
played. In 1995, the term 'involved in active play' was
included in the wording and this cut down the number of

occasions when play was stopped merely because someone happened to be in an offside position.

Has a goal ever been scored from a throw-in?

Barnsley's Frank Bokas scored directly from a throw during an FA Cup tie of January 1938. However the goal would have been disallowed if the ball hadn't touched the fingers of Manchester United goalkeeper Tommy Breen.

Wasn't there an experiment in which throw-ins were replaced with kick-ins?

This was tried in the Diadora League during season 1994–95. It didn't prove very popular.

Can a goal be scored from a corner?

Originally a goal wasn't allowed direct from a corner but that rule was changed in 1924. In October that year, Billy Smith of Huddersfield Town became the first player to take advantage of the new regulation.

Can a corner-flag be of any height?

No, it must be at least five feet high.

Are goal nets compulsory?

Not for minor matches. The invention of nets is credited to Mr J Brodie of Liverpool in 1890 and they were first introduced the following year.

What weight should the ball be?

The ball should weigh between 14 and 16 ounces at the start of the match.

Should a player be allowed to take part in a match if he is wearing a plaster?
It would depend on whether the referee considered it to be a danger to the other players. The 1978 World Cup final was nearly postponed after Argentina complained about a cast on the arm of Dutch star Rene van de Kerkhof.

TV has often shown a volleyed goal scored from an indirect free-kick which had been flicked up by a 'donkey-style' backheel. Why have we never seen that happen again?
The goal in question was scored by Coventry's Ernie Hunt from Willie Carr's flick during a First Division match against Everton in October 1970. Carr's trick has since been declared illegal.

During the 1997 Premiership match between Arsenal and Liverpool, 'Pool's Robbie Fowler tried to persuade the referee not to award a penalty for David Seaman's challenge on him. Was that the first time that has happened?
A similar sort of situation occurred in 1988 when German player Frank Ordenewicz was eventually bestowed with the FIFA Fair Play prize for persuading the referee to give a penalty AGAINST his own team.

What would be the referee's decision if a goalkeeper took a goal-kick which left the penalty area but was then blown back into the net by a strong wind?
In a case such as that, the ref should award a corner to the opposing team.

Is it possible for a player to score three goals in succession without anyone else touching the ball?
Yes, technically it's possible but it involves a complicated and unlikely scenario. Firstly Player A scores an own goal. Then he kicks off by launching a high ball into the opposition penalty-area. Before anyone has played the ball, one of his team-mates is tripped in the box and a penalty is awarded which Player A converts, just before the whistle blows for half-time! His team have the kick-off for the second half and exactly the same thing happens again. There, I told you it was complicated!

SUBSTITUTES

Who was the first-ever substitute?
Wales are believed to have made football's first-ever
substitution when they replaced their goalkeeper Gillam
with another, A Pugh, during a 1889 international against
Scotland at Wrexham. However, the concept of official
substitutes wasn't adopted until the 1960s.

What happened prior to the introduction of substitutes?
If a player left the field through injury, his team simply had
to play on with fewer men.

When were substitutes first introduced?
The Football League accepted the idea of substitutes, for
injured players only, in 1965 and Keith Peacock of Charlton
became English football's first sub when he took the field
against Bolton Wanderers in August that year. The Scottish
FA followed suit a year later and Archie Gemmill, then of St
Mirren, was Scottish football's first active No.12.

Who was the first substitute to score a League goal?
That was Bobby Knox for Barrow against Wrexham in
August 1965.

Has a substitute ever scored in an FA Cup final?
The first to do so was Eddie Kelly in the 1971 final against
Liverpool. No sub scored again until 1989 when my Rangers
mate Stuart McCall netted both of Everton's goals in their
3–2 defeat by Merseyside rivals Liverpool. Co-incidentally,
Reds' sub Ian Rush also scored twice in that game.

When was the number of substitutes increased to two and then three?
Two subs were allowed in international matches from 1967 onwards and, although that ruling was adopted in Scotland in 1973, it wasn't until season 1987–88 that the Football League introduced the idea. Since 1995, the International Board has permitted three substitutions to be made by each team during the course of a match.

When did substitutes first appear in the World Cup finals?
1970. During that year's final, Italy's goalscorer Roberto Boninsegna was replaced by Gianni Rivera.

Who was the first substitute to score in a World Cup final?
That was Holland's Dick Nanninga against Argentina in 1978. Apparently Nanninga had been telling reporters all week that he would come on and score.

Wasn't there a Hungarian substitute who scored a hat-trick in the World Cup finals?
Laszlo Kiss notched three goals in a nine-minute spell not long after taking the field in a 1982 first round match against El Salvador.

Is that the most outstanding performance by a sub in a major international tournament?
I would say yes. West Germany's Dieter Muller also scored a hat-trick against Yugoslavia in the semi-final of the 1976 European Championship, but two of his goals came in extra-time.

What's the fastest-ever international goal by a substitute?
That's credited to the former Arsenal player John Jensen who netted just five seconds after coming on for Denmark in a European Championship qualifier against Belgium in October 1994.

Has a sub ever been sent off before he has even had a kick of the ball?
That happened to Stoke's John Ritchie in 1972 and Bobby Houston of Kilmarnock in 1979. More recently, Bologna's Giuseppe Lorenzo lasted only ten seconds of his team's December 1990 Italian League match at Parma.

Who was the Republic of Ireland substitute who became involved in a huge row with the match officials during the 1994 World Cup finals?
It was John Aldridge who wasn't too chuffed when his entrance was delayed during the match against Mexico. It all worked out well enough in the end since Aldo headed what was to prove a vital goal.

Borussia Dortmund substitute Lars Ricken scored his side's decisive third goal in the 1997 Champions League final. Was it his first touch of the match?
Yes it was. Ricken replaced Stephane Chapuisat in the 70th minute and found the Juventus net within a minute of taking the field.

Who was the Liverpool player dubbed 'Supersub'?
That was David Fairclough who made 36 of his 64 appearances for the club as a substitute and also cultivated a habit of scoring vital goals. His greatest moment came in the 1977 European Cup quarter-final against St Etienne when he went on late in the second half and netted the goal which took The Reds through to the semis.

What's the shortest period of time that a sub has been involved in a match?
Arsenal 12th man Brian Hornby is reckoned to have taken the field in a 1973 match which had just three seconds remaining – not a great deal of time to make an impact!

Have four substitutes ever scored in a League game?
That happened during Barnet's 5–4 win over Torquay in
December 1992. Carter and Evans were the men on target for
Barnet while subs Trollope and Darby both netted for
Torquay.

DID YOU KNOW?

⚽ The first substitute to appear in a competitive match for
Rangers was Davie Wilson who replaced fellow winger
Willie Henderson in a League Cup sectional tie at
Kilmarnock in September 1966.

⚽ During the 1986 England-Scotland match, Gary Stevens
(of Everton) was replaced by Gary Stevens (of Spurs).

⚽ Chris Waddle was substituted 20 times in his 62
appearances for England between 1985 and 1991. On the
other hand, 14 of his caps were won as a sub.

⚽ Rangers' Ukrainian star Alexei Mikhailitchenko proved a
not-so-super sub in March 1994 when he FELL ASLEEP
while sitting on the bench during the Gers' Premier
League match at Hearts.

⚽ A rare type of substitution was made during the
Bulgaria–Mexico World Cup tie of 1994. The game was
delayed for several minutes when one of the goal-frames
was broken by a Mexican defender and had to be
replaced.

OFF DAYS

Are there much more sendings-off in football nowadays?
There's no question. In 1996–97, a total of 306 players were dismissed in English League football – compare that with an average of around 12 per season in the years immediately after the Second World War.

Has any player ever been ordered off in an FA Cup final at Wembley?
Manchester United's Kevin Moran is the only one to date. He was dismissed during the 1985 final against Everton.

Who was the first player to be shown a red card in the World Cup finals?
The first man sent off was Peru captain Mario De Las Casas against Romania in 1930. However the card system wasn't introduced until 1970 and Chile's Carlos Caszely was the first to see red, against West Germany in 1974.

Was Diego Maradona ever ordered off in a World Cup finals match?
Yes, as a 21-year-old in 1982. Maradona lost his head after a decision went against him and recklessly sunk his boot into the groin of a Brazilian opponent.

Which World Cup tournaments have seen the most and least dismissals?
Italia '90 set a new record of 16 sendings-off. There were no dismissals at all during the 1950, 1958 or 1970 finals.

Scotland took part in a World Cup match when there was a very early ordering-off. Who was the player involved?
It was Uruguay's Jose Batista who was shown the red card by French referee Joel Quiniou after just 55 seconds of the 1986 first round match in Mexico. Batista's dismissal remains the fastest sending-off in World Cup history.

What's the fastest sending-off of all time in British football?
Crewe goalkeeper Mark Smith was red-carded after just 19 seconds of a Third Division match at Darlington in March 1994.

Hearts had four players ordered off in a 1996 Premier League match at Ibrox. Was that the first time that four players from one team had been red-carded?
I came on as a sub in that game and it felt very strange to play against seven men. However, the first such instance in British football happened in September 1992 when four Hereford players were dismissed at Northampton.

Can a match continue if any more than four players from one side are sent off?
No, the rules state that a team must have at least seven players. In a Rio State League match of November 1991, a goal by Itaperuna resulted in no less than FIVE players of opponents America Tres Rios being ordered for dissent. The tie was abandoned and the points awarded to Itaperuna.

What's the highest number of dismissals in a completed match?
Unbelievably, EIGHT players (four from each team) were ordered off during the South American Super Cup quarter-final between Gremio of Brazil and Uruguay's Penarol in October 1993. Gremio won 2–0.

Has a player ever been allowed to stay on the field after being red-carded?

I actually took part in a match where that happened – the 1986 Old Firm Skol Cup final. Moments after Mo Johnston (then of Celtic) had been sent off, referee David Syme felt something strike him on the back of the head. Believing that Celtic's Tony Shepherd had been the culprit, Mr Syme flashed his red card at the midfielder then quickly changed his mind when he found a coin lying on the pitch.

There have been occasions though when players have simply refused to leave the pitch, haven't there?

Indeed! I recall Pasquale Bruno having to be dragged off following his red card in a Torino-Juventus derby game and there's also a story from a German match of 1977–78 when Bochum's Jochen Abel refused to go after being sent off against Schalke. When a crowd riot began to look a possibility, the referee changed Abel's card to a yellow.

MIXED BAG

The Estonia-Scotland World Cup tie of October 1996 lasted only three seconds. Is that the shortest football game in history?
I thought we were just starting to look good in that match! It must be the shortest game in history though obviously it won't be in the official records. Incidentally, it used to be the case that when a match was abandoned, the teams would meet at a later date to play out the time remaining. This actually happened in Spain as recently as 1995 when their cup final was washed out after 79 minutes and the last 10 minutes and 36 seconds were contested three days later.

Has there ever been a footballer who played in glasses?
There have been several, though not in recent times. Probably the most famous player to wear glasses was Jef Jurion of Anderlecht and Belgium. Meanwhile, 1960s Rangers star Willie Henderson was so short-sighted that he once asked the time – to the Celtic bench!

What is 'The Pyramid'?
It's the system of minor English leagues, headed by the Conference, which feeds into the Football League.

Is there a world record for ball-juggling?
The record is held by a South Korean called Sam Ik who juggled the ball (or, as we say in Scotland, 'played keepie-uppie') for an incredible 18 hours and 11 minutes in March 1995. Word was that he wasn't too pleased when someone shouted 'Play it again, Sam'!

Which club side has made the most appearances at Wembley?
Liverpool played on the famous turf 31 times between 1950 and 1997. Manchester United's appearance in the 1997 Charity Shield match was their 29th visit to the Stadium.

Has a father-and-son pairing ever played in the same team?
That's happened a few times. Danish star Michael Laudrup played one game alongside his father Finn for Brondby in 1981 while the most recent case in English League football was in April 1990 when Ian Bowyer, then Hereford player-manager, picked himself and son Gary against Scunthorpe.

Is it true that Manchester United legend Denis Law scored the goal which relegated The Reds during the 1970s?
No, that's not strictly true. Playing for Manchester City, Denis scored a cheeky back-heeled goal to defeat relegation-threatened United at Old Trafford in their penultimate match of 1973–74. However, because of the way other results went, United would have gone down anyway.

Has anyone ever played senior football in all four of the home countries?
I know of one definite case – my former Rangers team-mate John McClelland. Besides his spell in the Scottish Premier, Northern Ireland international John was also on the books of Bangor, Cardiff City and several English clubs.

Is it true that Newcastle won a European trophy after finishing TENTH in the previous season's English championship. If so, how did that happen?
Although United went on to win the 1969 Fairs Cup, they definitely entered through the back door. Of the teams

above them in the league, Manchester United (2nd) and Leeds (4th) qualified for Europe as title holders while West Brom (8th) went into the Cup-Winners' Cup. In addition, Everton (5th), Tottenham (7th) and Arsenal (9th) were all prohibited from entering the Fairs Cup because of the English FA's one-club-per-city ruling.

That ruling seems a bit harsh. Was it not?
It was a throw-back to the original idea behind the Fairs Cup but it was tough on clubs whose league position had really merited a European spot.

What was the first major football pop record?
'Back Home' by the 1970 England World Cup squad. Written by Rangers fan Bill Martin, it reached No.1 in the charts.

When did 'Roy of the Rovers' make his debut?
The star striker of Melchester Rovers first appeared in the comic *Tiger* in 1954. He is estimated to have scored over 5,000 goals during his career – real story-book stuff!

AND FINALLY...

Five fab facts on Super Ally himself...

⚽ Ally began his career as a midfielder with St Johnstone and it was the Perth team's manager Alex Rennie who decided to try him as a striker.

⚽ He once had a chance to meet his musical hero Bruce Springsteen – but missed it by turning up late!

⚽ Besides holding Rangers' League goalscoring record, Ally is also the Scottish League's top marksman since the war.

⚽ Coisty skippered Rangers for the first time in a September 1992 Premier League match against Dundee United at Tannadice. Fittingly, he scored in a 4–0 Gers win.

⚽ In 1990 Ally finished fifth in a poll to determine 'the world's best-looking sportsman'. He claimed to be thrilled – until he found out that tennis star Ivan Lendl had finished above him!